Who Guards the Guardians?

D1452706

In the quest to meet the summit of our potential, it is my firm conviction that our American Constitution will serve future generations with all their complexities, as it has the current generation and the generations of our forebears.

RICHARD B. RUSSELL

THE RICHARD B. RUSSELL LECTURE SERIES

The Richard B. Russell Foundation and the University of Georgia have joined in establishing this lecture series to honor the late Senator Russell. The Richard B. Russell Lectures will extend through the 1980s, addressing the Bicentennial of the Federal Constitution and encompassing the Charter of the University of Georgia in 1785. The Russell Lectures are scheduled for each year during this decade, at which time a distinguished guest of the University of Georgia will present three addresses on some notable aspect of the Constitution.

Martin Shapiro

Who Guards the Guardians?
Judicial Control
of Administration

THE RICHARD B. RUSSELL LECTURES

NUMBER SIX

The University of Georgia Press

Athens and London

© 1988 by the University of Georgia Press
Athens, Georgia 30602
All rights reserved

Set in Palatino
The paper in this book meets the guidelines for
permanence and durability of the Committee on
Production Guidelines for Book Longevity of the
Council on Library Resources.

Printed in the United States of America

92 91 90 89 88   5 4 3 2 1

Library of Congress Cataloging in Publication Data

Shapiro, Martin M.
    Who guards the guardians?

    (The Richard B. Russell lectures ; no. 6)
    Includes index.
    1. Judicial review of administrative acts—
United States. 2. Political questions and judicial
power—United States. I. Title. II. Series.
KF5425.S53 1988   342.73'0664   87-5927
ISBN 0-8203-0963-x (alk. paper) 347.302664

British Library Cataloging in Publication Data available.

TO DICK BRODY, BOB ROSENZWEIG, AND RAY WOLFINGER
with whom I shared farm chores about twenty-five years ago.

Contents

Preface

The aim of this book is to introduce to students of American politics and policy-making a segment of politics that concerns the relationship between administrative agencies and the courts that review them. Courts have been reviewing agencies for a long time. Why do we need an introduction now? We need it essentially because this area of political relationships has long been known as "administrative law" and administrative law has long been either unknown by students of politics or known as an impenetrable body of legal-doctrinal esoterica. Indeed, having spent many years confronting political science and public policy students who had no idea what administrative law was, except the idea that it was too technical to bother with, I now confront law students who come to my office to ask "Just what is administrative law?" before they sign up for my course. I never get that question when I teach constitutional law. Nor do tort and contract and tax teachers.

For those readers who fear the unknown, let me hasten to say that this is not a book on administrative law in the narrow sense. It does not present the marvelously prolific doctrinal learning of "primary jurisdiction" and the "arbitrary and capricious" standard of review. Instead, it is a book about the general ideas from which these esoteric doctrines flow. More precisely, it is a book about the changes in these ideas and the changes in court-agency relations flowing from them that have occurred in the last half century. Finally, it is primarily a book about how those ideas are changing right now and what those changes may mean for the political relations between courts and agencies in the next decade.

An introduction to this broader vision of what, in its doctrinal form, lawyers call "administrative law" and what the rest of us call judicial review of administrative action is timely now for two reasons, one having to do with the stage of development of the body of learning called political science–public administration–

public policy, the other having to do with the real world of politics. Let us take the real world first. In the 1970s and 1980s there has been a gigantic outburst of congressional statutes regulating health, safety, and the environment, all of which create an enormous sphere of action for the administrative agencies that implement them. In the eighties there has been a movement toward deregulation in some of the traditional areas of economic regulation which also creates new discretion in implementing agencies. For reasons this book will explain, courts have been important participants in the very complex policy processes entailed in these new regulations and deregulations. We used to speak of the "iron triangles" or "whirlpools" of congressional committee–interest group–administrative agency in the policy process. As Shep Melnick tells us, it is now better political geometry to speak of the "iron rectangle" of the subcommittee–interest group–administrative agency–court. Or, if you don't like geometry, we might simply say that courts have become major participants in the free-for-all of policy-making described by Hugh Heclo. And this major participation does *not* take the form of *constitutional* judicial review of whether the agency's action is or is not constitutional. It is *not* the Supreme Court doing those things that began with *Marbury* v. *Madison* of which "public law" political scientists are so fond. Instead it is *statutory* judicial review, mostly by district and circuit courts, which asks not whether the agency practice is unconstitutional, but only whether the agency practice is in accordance with the laws of Congress.

Now we come to the changes in learning. Political science–public administration passed through a "behavioral" phase. Because behaviorism saw itself as a reaction to an earlier excessive formalism, and law was a major part of that formalism, law as a subject of study within political science–public administration fell into a phase of retreat. Administrative law nearly disappeared from curricula, and "public law" in political science was reduced to "constitutional law." As behaviorism enriched even the study of public law, it was natural that the form of the enrichment was the study of Supreme Court justices' attitudes in constitutional law cases.

One major phenomenon occurred which broke the Supreme Court constitutional law ghetto of "public law." Behavioral political scientists studying not "public law" but "urban politics" began to look at what really went on in city politics. As they did so, they kept running into these things called trial courts which seemed to play a big part in urban politics, so those political scientists interested in courts added the study of the local criminal business of trial courts to their interest in the constitutional law of the Supreme Court. All of this created a peculiar political science which treated the most elevated constitutional decisions of the highest of the high courts and the most routine criminal trials of the lowest of the low courts and practically nothing in between. And it did nothing for public administration at all.

We have now supplemented our interest in behaviorism with a new concern for "public policy." So we have gotten the urban politics phenomenon all over again. "Public law" scholars kept on studying the constitutional decisions of the Supreme Court. But those studying both public policy-making and the actual substance of policy realized that courts seemed to have a great influence over what happened. Most of the courts involved were lower federal courts, not the Supreme Court, and most of the law involved was not constitutional law but statutory environmental, health, and safety law, as well as what lawyers called "administrative law." So at this very moment, political scientists concerned with courts are beginning to study the huge bodies of regulatory and administrative law and the federal district and circuit courts that enforce these laws—all of which they have largely ignored for years. And in both political science and public administration, administrative law courses are beginning to revive.

So both because the real world has changed and because the disciplines have changed, it is a good idea to look at some fundamental questions about how, when, and why courts should participate in politics, policy-making, and public administration by judicial review of the actions of administrative agencies.

There are two other reasons for this book at this time. One has to do with the newest of the catch phrases to take its place beside behaviorism and policy, *institutional analysis*. The new emphasis on institutional analysis tells us that in addition to individual political behavior and economic forces, we must pay attention to the long-term development of state institutions in relation to one another if we are to understand politics and administration. This book is about institutions—courts and administrative agencies—and how their relations have changed over time and are likely to change in the future.

Finally, I hope that this book is timely because it is an attempt to identify a new body of ideas to which I do not necessarily subscribe, but which I believe will be extremely important in determining our attitudes toward court-agency relations in the next several decades. I have used the word *deliberation* as the symbol or identifying flag for these ideas. It is important that students of political science and administration become aware of these ideas now, because for the next several years they will be the force behind much of the writing on public administration, policy-making, and administrative law.

This book is an expanded and modified version of my Richard B. Russell Lectures at the University of Georgia. My thanks are due to the Richard B. Russell Lectures Committee and its chair, Professor Lester B. Stephens, and particularly to Lief Carter and Frank Thompson, political scientists at Georgia who are fellow students of law and administration. I am also indebted to the deans and faculty of the University of California-Berkeley law school, who some years ago drafted me into the teaching of administrative law to law students, and to the subset of my law school colleagues who constitute the Jurisprudence and Social Policy Program and who keep insisting that I say something more interesting than what law students want to hear.

Chapter One

Deliberation

This book originated in the University of Georgia's Russell Lectures, devoted to the American Constitution. This particular set of Russell Lectures concerned the ways in which judges oversee the decisions of those who work in the administrative or executive branch of government. The book itself focuses upon one of the oldest political questions: Who guards the guardians? If we set judges to protect us from bureaucrats, how are we to protect ourselves from judges?

It is the duty of every citizen to watch and to evaluate the actions and policies of government. In the American tradition, we also set each part of government to watch the others and many nongovernmental institutions, such as the news media and interest groups, to keep watch as well. What are we watching for and how do we evaluate what we see? What makes a government decision good or bad, right or wrong? At the moment these questions are harder to answer than they might seem and harder to answer than they have been at some other times in our history. Yet if we are to set judges to watch bureaucrats, we must either tell the judges the answers to these questions or expect them to figure them out for themselves. It may be argued that judges are not as heavily burdened as other citizens, that they need not decide whether government acts are right or wrong, good or bad, but only whether such acts are lawful or unlawful, just or unjust. We shall see later, however, that when judges decide about the lawfulness or justness of administrative agency decisions, questions of right and good become inextricably tangled with questions of law and justice. In reality we have given the judges a task of surveillance not so different than that of the citizens in general. Judges cannot dodge these very difficult questions of rightness and goodness.

Answers to questions about the goodness or badness of a particular government action ultimately depend on whether we believe that political life in general ought to be devoted to the satisfaction of individual preferences or the attainment of moral principles. The current body of writing on judicial review of administrative action—what lawyers call "administrative law"—is clearly, directly, and often self-consciously linked to current developments in moral and political philosophy. So before we get to the judges themselves, we must look at these issues of preferences and principles.

Let us suppose for the moment that we believe it is impossible to discover a set of fundamental moral principles or values that can be used to guide and evaluate political action in a democracy. We might come to such a belief for a number of reasons. A review of the past efforts of moral philosophers might lead us to the conclusion that the discovery or formulation of a coherent set of such principles is beyond human capacity, or that many such sets of principles had been formulated by various persons at various times but none had achieved sufficient consensus to serve as a basis for governance. Yet another possibility is that the only such principles to achieve a sufficient consensus were necessarily so general that even those who agreed upon the principle could not agree whether a particular public policy was required, allowed, or forbidden by the principle. (We all believe in the principle that equals should be treated equally, but that does not lead to a moral consensus on affirmative action, for instance.) In short we might conclude that, at least as far as political life was concerned, we ought to think of every individual as having his or her own moral values which we ought to treat as nothing more than personal preferences. Whether a particular government policy was right or wrong would depend on how many people preferred it to some alternative policy.

Such a position is not identical to the claim that in politics every person is an entirely selfish being seeking only to maximize his or her "power" or material benefits. Indeed, this "preference" stance toward politics does not depend upon any particular vision of human nature as selfish or altruistic or even of the universe as a cosmos governed by rules or a chaos. It rests only on an interpretation of human history that sees humans as unable to generate an agreed set of basic principles from which indisputably correct public policies can be deduced. As a result we treat politics as having to do with aggregating or choosing among individual preferences, rather than finding and following moral principles.

An alternative view of the moral history of mankind and an alternative approach to ethics teaches that human values are not mere preferences, mere statements that "I like vanilla" and "You like chocolate." Instead, there are objective values in the sense of some ultimate goal of the good person in the good state and/or in the sense of some do's and don'ts that are morally binding at all times. If a particular public policy leads us away from our ultimate vision of the good, or if it violates one of our do's and don'ts, then it is a bad public policy. The goodness or badness of a law or other government action does not depend on how many people want it but on whether it is objectively right or wrong.

From about 1930 to 1970 most Americans who devoted themselves to thinking and writing about law and politics relied upon the former, or "preference," vision. The dominant school of moral philosophy was utilitarianism, drawn from the writings of Jeremy Bentham. Bentham sought to derive a moral philosophy by what he thought of as a purely empirical and scientific mode of inquiry. He began from a purely factual premise of human behavior or psychology—all people seek pleasure and shun pain. From that premise he derived a moral premise: every act is good to the degree that it increases the sum of human pleasure and bad to the degree that it increases the sum of pain. From there it is but a step to a political morality. A government action is good or bad depending upon whether or not it achieves the greatest good for the greatest number of persons. Or to put the matter in slightly different words, every act is to be judged by its consequences in terms of how many benefits it will bring at what costs.

In a sense, utilitarianism, too, offered an objective moral standard, "the greatest good of the greatest number." To the utilitarian, however, no act or government policy was good in and of itself but was good only on the basis of its consequences in creating more or less of what they wanted for more or fewer people. And any action, no matter how adverse to a particular individual, might be justified on the basis that the detriment to some individuals was outweighed by the advantages to others. The objective ethical principle that utilitarianism offered was that there were no such principles except satisfying the preferences of individuals. So the only right thing to do was to give as many people what they wanted as you could. Modern economics is a branch of utilitarianism, and it offers an especially precise formulation of the basic utilitarian principle called "Paretan optimality." Paretan optimality is a distribution of whatever is valued by individuals in such a way that any change in the distribution would make fewer people better off than it would make worse off.

Utilitarianism and American democracy appear to be compatible in many ways. Every voter can be seen as having a set of preferences. Elections are mechanisms for summating these preferences and giving the majority what they want. Any government and any government action approved by majority vote must, almost by definition, be right because it will give the greater number what they prefer.

Pluralist Political Theory

In the period immediately preceding and following World War II, political scientists began to stress that democratic politics was centered less in individual voting than in group political activity. Politics consisted of interest groups struggling with one another for access to the levers of power.[1] This pluralist, or "polyarchical," vision of politics was compatible with utilitarianism. What defined a set of individuals as an interest group was that they shared a particular set of preferences. The process of making public policy consisted of groups competing with one another for what legislators, administrative agencies, and courts had to offer. The result of this group struggle would be an aggregation or summating of group preferences in the way that elections summated individual preferences. Any government action achieved by a group struggle in which all the relevant groups participated would be right almost by definition, because it would reflect the interests of the greater number of groups.

The group theory of politics is today offered in two slightly different forms, one derived from political science and the other from economics. The political theorists who propounded pluralist or polyarchical views did not necessarily imply that there was no such thing as the common good or public interest as opposed to the sum of individual or group interests. They did not explicitly argue that there was no ideal of the good person in the good state toward which public policy should be directed or that there were no absolute or deontological rights or wrongs. They did argue, however, that there was no universally accepted logical or scientific procedure for determining the good and relatively little consensus on what the good was. Each group would have its own necessarily incomplete and somewhat distorted vision of the public good. Given these realities, and as a second-best solution in the absence of universally agreed right policies, the pluralists were driven toward a proceduralist criterion as a working standard for public policy. Those public policies were to be considered correct that were arrived at by a process in which all relevant groups had actively participated, each with enough political clout to insure that its views had to be taken into account by the ultimate decision makers.

Such a pluralist, procedural criterion could be taken in one of two ways. It could mean that, in the absence of any more objective way of determining political truth, the clash and compromise of various groups, each with its own vision of the public good, was the best available means of approximating that good. Taken in this way, pluralism is not a denial that there are good and bad, or at least better and worse, public policies, perhaps even quite apart from the greatest good for the greatest number. The pluralist need not be taken as saying that politics is merely the aggregation of group preferences devoid of any component of a more absolute or general good. He may be insisting only that the best political process for achieving the good is one that allows for the clash of competing visions of the good.

Pluralism may be viewed another way, however, as in the case of many economists who have turned it into a theory of "public choice."[2] The most successful branch of economics has been microeconomics, which has developed a very elegant and persuasive theory of how individuals make decisions to buy and sell in "markets"—that is, in situations wherein such decisions are made by individuals acting independently. Economists have recognized that in any society there are also many nonmarket decisions that must be made collectively rather than by individuals, such as the decision to enact a law. Given the success of microeconomic theory, it has been an obvious task of economists to see how much of that theory, invented for markets, could also be made to work for nonmarket choices.

It is also fairly obvious how the group theory of politics could help in the application of microeconomic theory to political or public choices. The legislature or other political arena is seen as a kind of market. Each group enters the market seeking to get government policy that will favor its own interests and pays for such policy by giving votes or campaign contributions or other political support to the law makers. In legislative bodies that operate by majority voting, a number of groups will use "logrolling" to form a "minimum winning coalition." In other words, a number of groups will cooperate with one another, each supporting the interests of some other groups in exchange for their supporting its interests. As soon as enough of these groups have coalesced to win 51 percent of the legislative votes, this coalition will get legislation passed embodying its various interests. The legislation will not embody the interests of any nonmember groups because their political resources are not necessary to gain the majority of legislative votes needed to pass the bill.

Once the bill is passed, the particular coalition of groups ends. Each group is again free to form new coalitions for passing other bills. Legislative markets will tend toward efficiency. That is, they will give each group the minimum amount of what it wants in order to gain its support for what other groups want. Group politics or pluralism will yield, therefore, statutes that embody neither a general or common good nor even the greatest good for the greatest number of groups. Instead, legislative markets yield statutes that supply the least good necessary to recruit the smallest number of groups that can form a winning coalition on a particular issue. In theory, all groups will get something because each will be sometimes in winning and sometimes in losing coalitions.

Of course, even in the economists' vision, some legislation might sometimes embody some elements of a more general interest. In private market situations individuals may sometimes be willing to pay for something that benefits others or that benefits everyone equally, as they do for instance when they make charitable contributions. So, too, in the realm of public choice, some groups may choose at times to lend their political support to government policies that would help others or everyone. Even if individual and group moral life is never anything more than the pursuit of preferences, the preferences of individuals and groups need not always be narrowly selfish ones. Sometimes we actually prefer to help others rather than ourselves or to purchase certain goods, like medical research or military defense, that serve everyone rather than only ourselves.

Nevertheless, in this economic vision, most legislation, particularly when it regulates economic activity, is essentially a matter of creating and allocating "rents." For instance, a barbers' group goes to a state legislature and gets a law passed requiring that no one can work as a barber unless he or she gets a state license granted only after a tough exam. The result is a smaller number of barbers than there would otherwise be. The result of having a smaller number of barbers is a higher price for haircuts. The difference between what licensed barbers charge for a haircut and the lower price they would charge if there were more competition from more barbers is a rent. This unearned income or rent is created and assigned to them by the licensing statute. Most group politics will consist of groups exchanging their political support for votes from legislators on bills that will get them more than they could get in a free market in the absence of legislation. Thus, while in theory leaving some room for the pursuit of the common good, group politics as presented by economists is even more oriented to partial and selfish interests than is the pluralism of political scientists.

Political theories of pluralism are usually expressed in terms of access and influence. Those groups that can gain access to policymakers use that access to seek to persuade them that the policies favored by the group should be adopted by the government. Some of this access and influence is pure exchange. The group gains the ear of the policymaker by saying, "if you will listen to us and then do what we say, we will vote for you, or contribute to your campaign or support some policy you want." Often, however, access and influence may be based on the perception of policymakers that they and an interest group share a desire to achieve the common good and can achieve that good by cooperation. Thus a "Union of Concerned Scientists" may gain access to a Senate committee by saying, "We both want to solve the problem of nuclear waste, and we scientists have the expertise to tell you how. So listen to us." And the union of scientists may actually influence the committee's decision because the senators believe that the scientists have the expert knowledge to solve the common problem.

Economic group theories tend to emphasize pure exchange elements. Government policymakers are thought to pursue their own selfish interest, such as getting reelected, and interest groups are regarded in the same way. The policymakers will give the groups the policies they want if, in exchange, the groups give the policymakers the political support they need in order to get reelected or keep their administrative agencies going. More politically oriented group theories leave more room for collaboration between groups and government decision makers to achieve shared visions of the public good.

It is not difficult to imagine the first set of objections to be made to group theories of politics. In free markets, goods are allocated to individuals on the basis of what price they will pay.

Prices are set by supply and demand under competitive conditions. Such markets do a perfect job of satisfying everyone's preferences so long as everyone starts with the same amount of money with which to pay the prices. Even if life is merely individual preferences, the free market, viewed only as a distribution mechanism, is not fair or just if some people have a lot more money than others. Similarly, even where government policy is seen as only the satisfaction of group interests that compete freely for government favor, the result will not be considered fair and just if some groups have a great deal more political power than others. If some groups control a large number of votes, or can make large campaign contributions, or have other political resources, they can "pay" more and thus wield more access and influence than other groups. So they will get more of their preferences enacted into law or other government policy.

The first critical response to pluralism was, therefore, an emphasis on the fact that the group struggle would yield public policies that favored some groups over others simply because some groups were more politically influential than others. The result might be quite at odds with the preferences of a majority of the individual citizens and not in accord with the greatest good of the greatest number.

Later we shall look at some of the inventions that administrative law threw up to meet this criticism. For the moment it is enough to say that the first response was a whole set of devices designed to equalize the position in the policy "market" of the competing interests. In many instances, large numbers of people shared an interest but had not organized into groups that could compete effectively. During the 1960s and 1970s, there was a great deal of effort to organize neighborhood residents, the elderly, the poor, consumers, nature lovers, members of racial and linguistic minorities, and others into effective political groups. Simply organizing often gave these groups considerable political influence because, once organized, they could call on their members for votes, money, and personal action in support of group political goals.

Various efforts have also been made to increase group access to administrative agencies and courts by providing some of them with government-funded legal services and other kinds of support funded by government and private foundations. The Freedom of Information Act and various "sunshine" acts were passed to make it easier for groups that do not have good "inside" contacts to find out what is happening in government. Then they are in a better position to present their cases to the right government decision makers at the right time.

All of these are attempts to level up, to give more access and influence to the weaker groups. There have also been attempts to level down. For instance, the sunshine acts that require government bodies to make their decisions in public do provide more needed information for groups without government friends to tell them what is going on. In addition, these acts are designed to limit the influence of the most powerful groups by exposing their dealings with government agencies to public scrutiny. The Campaign Financing Act and other statutes that limit campaign contributions and spending and provide government funds to candidates are designed to reduce the power of big money groups.

In spite of all the tinkerings of the last three decades, however, there remains great discontent with a pluralist political process. Some groups are obviously far more equal than others. Above all is the fear that certain powerful groups will "capture" administrative agencies or congressional committees or courts and run the government. A part of government that constantly hears from one powerful group that offers to help the agency if the agency will just do what the group defines as right is likely, over the years, to take on the group's point of view as its own.

Some allegedly captured agencies are sometimes "liberated." Ecologists now have a major voice in Forest Service decisions that once appeared to be dominated by timber-cutting interests. Deregulation has tried to solve the problem of capture of certain agencies by simply doing away with the agency's power to help those who might have held it captive. The Civil Aeronautics Board may have been the captive of the airlines. Airline deregulation means that no federal agency can any longer grant particular airlines exclusive routes and high rates. Many of the new agencies, such as the Environmental Protection Agency and the Occupational Safety and Health Administration, regulate all industries rather than a particular one. Agencies like the Civil Aeronautics Board that regulated a single industry were obvious targets for capture; that industry would work very hard to influence the agency. An agency that regulates all industries is not easily captured by any one of them.

Nevertheless, far greater influence of some groups than others over certain government agencies, frequently amounting to something like capture, is still perceived to be a major problem of American politics. The constant concern about the web of relations between defense contractors, Defense Department procurement agencies and the relevant congressional committees is the most obvious example.

For a time it seemed that the only response to the perceived inequalities of pluralism—the picture of powerful groups capturing agencies in order to help themselves against less powerful rival groups—would be more pluralism. We would undertake the organization of more groups and the assignment of more resources to the weaker ones.[3] The competition of relatively equal rival groups for influence over a given part of government would prevent any one of them from achieving capture.

It seems unlikely that such superpluralist moves would have fully satisfied the antipluralist critiques no matter what else was happening. Something else, however, was happening. Pluralism was highly compatible with the brand of ethics that conceived of values as essentially matters of personal preference. The critique of pluralism might have been regarded as only making the point that group processes in America did not result in government policies that accurately aggregated the preferences of all groups. The more politically powerful groups got too much of what they preferred and the weaker ones too little. If that had been the only ethical basis of the attack on pluralism, the response from pluralists would have been, "Group processes may not perfectly aggregate preferences but they are the best way we've got to aggregate preferences." Something of a standoff would have been reached.

Just at the time when attacks on pluralism reached their peak, however, a new development in ethics was occurring that allowed antipluralists to make out a far more positive case for an alternative to pluralism than simply that pluralism did not work perfectly because of group inequality. Beginning in the 1960s, a major movement has occurred in moral philosophy that has been labelled "postconsequentialist" ethics. It rejects utilitarianism in favor of an emphasis on the value of an act quite apart from its consequences.[4]

Postconsequentialist Ethics

This alternative or postconsequentialist ethics may insist that acts are good and bad in and of themselves because they are in accordance with or violate moral rules like "Thou Shalt Not Kill." These moral rules are taken to be valid quite apart from their consequences. Such an ethic is said to assert "deontological" values. Or postconsequentialist ethics may be based on the notion that political life is informed by a vision of what the good life would ultimately be in the good society or the good state. The goodness or badness of a particular act depends upon whether it moves us toward or away from that vision. Such an ethics is said to be "teleological." Of course, it is not purely nonconsequentialist. It does look to the consequences of an act to determine its rightness or wrongness. It is asking about consequences, however, not in terms of giving most people what they immediately prefer but in terms of an ultimate goal. That ultimate goal of the good person leading the good life in the good state is not a matter of personal preferences. The teleologist is actually measuring current acts against some ideal and the content of that ideal is determined in some way other than aggregating preferences. Moral persons must think out what the ideal society would look like and measure the ethical quality of current acts in accordance with their contribution to that ideal.

Both varieties of nonconsequentialist ethics are antiutilitarian.

They refuse to accept "the greatest good for the greatest number," particularly in the form "the greatest preferences of the greatest number" as the central tenant of public ethics. When these sorts of antiutilitarian ethics are added to the initial attack on pluralism, they provide a much more positive thrust to that attack.

Basing themselves on the interest in reviving deontological and teleological ethics to be found in the new breed of postutilitarian or postconsequentialist philosophers, antipluralists could now move to a new position. They could argue that even if group struggle were the best available way in an imperfect world to aggregate personal preferences, the goodness or badness of a government action ought not to be solely a question of aggregate personal preferences or the greatest good for the greatest number. We also ought to ask whether proposed government actions are right or wrong in the deontological sense. Do they or do they not violate basic moral rules? And we ought to ask of every government action whether it contributes merely to the immediate selfish interests of some or many or to the common good or the general welfare in the sense of moving us toward a better society for everyone? In short, the key public policy question is not how many groups want it but whether it is right or wrong. If that is the question, then mere tinkering with the groups to even them up is not the route to political virtue.

Thus, increasingly, we are coming to believe that government policy should be judged not only as to its process but as to its substance. We are no longer content to say that, because everyone has his or her own ideas of right and wrong, the only good public policy is one which every relevant group participated in forming. If all the groups took part in the ecological plan, but all the fish in the river died, we are not prepared to say that the plan was right. But what criteria of substantive, as opposed to procedural, right and wrong are we to use? And what procedures are we to use for establishing such substantive criteria of right and wrong? These are the questions that have begun to beckon to the critics of pluralism. Perhaps they provide a way out of the frustration of being able to propose no cure for the pathologies of pluralism except more pluralism—that is, the creation of more groups and more equalization of group resources.

"Rationality" as a Cure for Pluralism

Not surprisingly, one of the very first routes chosen for establishing substantive criteria of right and wrong for government policy was utilitarianism itself. It may appear something of a paradox that one of the first vehicles of postconsequentialist urges should be an appeal to that most preference-oriented and most consequentialist philosophy. The greatest good for the greatest number, however, particularly as translated by economists into the concept of economic efficiency, is a very useful tool lying ready to hand for the critics of pluralism. If the processes of group politics at any given moment yield public policies that are not economically efficient, such as subsidies to tobacco farmers, then those policies are substantively wrong even if the groups all struggled vigorously.

Economists have both optimistic and pessimistic readings of the phenomenon. Some say that over time the competition and logrolling of the groups will lead to economically efficient policies, that is, policies that provide optimum satisfaction for the preferences that actually exist in the society. Groups that want something badly enough will keep fighting until they get it and will give in to other groups on things the other groups want the most. Other economists are prone to argue that such efficiency would result only if there were perfectly free and equal group competition in a political market perfectly structured to respond accurately to all expressions of group preference. Many of them argue that, in fact, existing political processes and institutions tend to heavily overweigh some groups and their preferences and underweigh others. Even the optimists agree that no matter what the long term overall outcome, many public policies proposed or in place today are substantively wrong in the sense of being economically inefficient.[5]

So far, we have been talking about economic efficiency at a

kind of wholesale level. What would provide the most benefits for the society as a whole at the least cost? More narrowly we may speak of "rationality" in the economist's sense. Leaving aside the ultimate question of what would be optimal for the whole country, let us begin with some set of preferences that we have agreed to seek to achieve. A "rational" policy is the one that yields us the most of what we prefer at the least cost. Surely, no matter what our views about ethics are, all of us can agree that it is better to achieve the good efficiently rather than inefficiently, at the lowest possible cost, not the highest. This concept of economic rationality or efficiency can serve as a substantive criterion of goodness or badness for public policy and also suggests a procedure for arriving at substantive good. At least once the goal is specified, a good public policy is one that achieves the goal "rationally" or "efficiently," that is, at the least cost. The appropriate procedure for identifying the good policy is essentially oriented to information and technology. If the policymakers find all the facts and identify all the possible alternative ways of reaching the agreed goal, then they can choose the least costly alternative. We would all agree that the most efficient alternative is best.

One solution, therefore, for many of those dissatisfied with group struggle is to turn to rationality or efficiency as criteria for public policy and rational or synoptic decision-making processes as the best decision-making processes. By synoptic we simply mean a process that gathers all the facts, considers all alternative policies and all the possible consequences of each, and chooses those policies with the highest probability of achieving agreed goals at least cost. Such procedures have been widely adopted as reforms designed to give us better public policies. "Program," "zero-based," and other budgeting techniques, environmental and regulatory impact statements and regulatory analyses, and statutes that specify that agencies make rules on the basis of "the best available evidence" or "substantial evidence on the rule-making record as a whole" are examples of recent tendencies to move away from group struggle and toward "rational" decision making. In these instances it is not the product of group struggle but the product of rational economic and technical analysis that is, by definition, good policy.[6]

This renewed confidence in rationality is only a very partial solution to most pluralist problems, however, because it retains the weakness of utilitarianism at the ultimate ethical level. Synoptic decision processes can work only if we can agree on precisely what goals or values the policy we are seeking is to serve and exactly what the priority among those goals is if there are more than one. So the ultimate ethical problem of specifying basic values remains.

Even utilitarians who are satisfied with the greatest good for the greatest number as their basic value have trouble with synoptic decision making at this point. For in recent years it has been demonstrated that, if many individuals or groups have different preferences, there is no democratic process such as voting that will allow us to summate these preferences into a single correct greatest-good-for-the-greatest-number policy outcome.[7] This "paradox" of voting means that different individuals will get more or less of what they want depending on certain accidents or structures of the decision-making process. No decision-making process is perfect. If some of us want A, some B, and some C, it often turns out that there is no way of arriving at just that mix of A, B, and C that would be the greatest good for the greatest number. This problem is especially acute when some of those who want A want it twice as much as they want B and B twice as much as C and others who want A would just as soon have C but really hate B. If there is no rational process for specifying values that can cope with the variety of preferences and the variety of intensity of preferences, then true synopticism is never possible. For we can never arrive by rational processes at the single exactly correct specification of goals and goal priorities that synopticism requires.

The world of politics is not an all-or-nothing one. Those fond of utilitarian approaches reply to the kind of arguments just made that in many public policy areas there is relatively high agreement about goals. Moreover, even when some prefer A, some B, and some C, and no single correct mix of A, B, and C can be rationally derived, some mixes of A, B, and C obviously come closer than others to meeting our preferences. For instance, choosing D is clearly wrong. Better to choose one of six equally plausible mixtures of A, B, and C as our goal than some other that is clearly less compatible with our preferences. Synopticism directed at achieving any one of the several different mixes of values that come somewhere close to the ideal greatest good for the greatest number appears to many like a better course of action than catch-as-catch-can group bargaining for policy outcome.

Utilitarians in general and economists in particular even have a way of incorporating contemporary urges toward deontological and teleological values. Even if the moral world is nothing but individual preferences, an individual may prefer teleological or ontological values. It may give X great pain to see Y deprived of his property without due process of law. It may give both X and Y great pain to discover that they have been outvoting Z consistently and as a result, Z never gets any of what he wants. In short, among the greatest goods that the greatest number may want may well be certain levels of equality and of rights for those who are not among the greatest number. And, of course, the greatest number may share some ideal picture of the perfect society of the future. If so, policies that move society toward this shared teleological value will give great pleasure to the greatest numbers. Utilitarianism can handle altruism and all sorts of nonutilitarian values by translating them into preferences. Humans can suffer pains and pleasures to their philosophies as well as to their stomachs.

For many postpluralists, however, this kind of utilitarian translation of ultimate values back into personal preferences is an undervaluing of values. It makes procedural errors because it makes substantive errors. For the utilitarian, public values are simply the greatest value preferences of the greatest number. If the substance of human values is simply the preferences of individuals for one or another set of values, then the procedure for establishing the values that are to inform government policies must remain some kind of aggregation of those preferences. The process for such aggregation will be markets, voting, group struggle, or the like. To many persons concerned with ethics, it seems unlikely that deontological or teleological moral truth is to be found by the majority vote of people who have not thought seriously about value questions. Voting and other methods of simply aggregating preferences entail asking value questions in a rapid and casual way that appears unlikely to lead to moral truth, because moral truth is not ultimately a matter of unexamined personal preference.

Discourse

What procedures would postconsequentialist philosophers and the postpluralists who look to those philosophers find appropriate for discovering the values that are to guide government decisions about public policy? To find out, we must first discover what procedures they believe philosophers themselves ought to employ in discovering ethical truth. For anyone not a professional philosopher, it is quite difficult to understand how the new moral philosophers do what they do. It is even more difficult to convey the spirit and style of what they do to other nonprofessionals. We must try to understand, however, because there is really a very substantial contemporary push to get this style inserted into governmental decision-making processes. And, as we shall see later, many descriptions of the style suggest that judges would be particularly good at it.

The central feature of the new ethics appears to be discourse.[8] Philosophers arrive at postconsequentialist values by speaking and writing to one another. This communication is not usually conceived of as some sort of formal debate. Rather it should be a collective, collaborative discussion among philosophers that proposes and tests moral propositions. Its outstanding feature is that everyone must speak carefully and precisely. It is the stock-in-trade of all modern philosophy that words do not have single absolutely fixed meanings, so there is always a certain ambiguity about human communication. All the more reason to use words and frame issues as carefully and unambiguously as possible. Ethical discourse should not only be conducted to reduce verbal misunderstanding as much as possible, it should also be logical. As contradictions or missing steps in reasoning are identified, they should be fixed. Discourse is not afraid to rest on what is probable when it cannot know things for certain, and it employs the set of modern techniques developed for dealing with probabilities.

Most importantly, when dealing with moral questions, discourse aims at persuasion rather than proof. The new moral philosophers believe that those who reject the notion that there are true moral values do so because of a fundamental error. Just because one cannot prove a moral value the way one proves a theorem in geometry or a fact ought not to mean that we abandon the search for values. We cannot conclude that, because no value is absolutely true or can be proved with total certainty, we should treat values as mere personal preferences. The new moral discourse seeks to arrive at an agreement that certain moral positions are more true than other propositions. The talk is not ended by a vote on which propositions discussed are truest, nor does consensus prove that the proposition that has achieved consensus is true. As soon as one of the talkers can offer a persuasive objection to a principle on which consensus appears to have been reached, talk will begin again, aimed at a more persuasive formulation. It is extremely difficult to convey the style of this talk, but it is a curious and wonderful mixture of appeals to logic, to experience, and above all, to very carefully examined and criticized, but nonetheless deeply held convictions that certain ways of treating human beings are revolting to our deepest moral senses. A process of careful, logical reasoning together is central to the ethical enterprise.

Having said all this, we cannot quite have captured the essence of the postconsequentialist movement. Some of us might suppose that ten philosophers might speak together carefully for ten years and not come up with a set of moral values that were self-evidently true. What happens when the philosophers reach a disagreement about a value question that cannot be resolved simply by clearing up linguistic misunderstandings and logical flaws? The postconsequentialists forbid us to call them intuitionists. Intuitionism is an earlier and now outmoded approach to philosophy. Nevertheless, it is difficult for outsiders not to say that when postconsequentialists have cleared away misunderstandings and reached a real moral issue, they decide the issue by resorting to their moral intuitions.

Postconsequentialists say otherwise. They say that when true moral issues are uncovered and carefully stated, the participants in moral discourse are able to discern some moral resolutions that are far more persuasive, appealing or correct than others. The participants in such discourse insist that they do not simply add up or try for a consensus about their moral hunches. Instead, by the very process of discourse itself, they arrive at statements of moral values that are persuasive even if they cannot be proven to be absolutely correct. These statements might take the form of general moral rules to guide individual and political life. Or they might take the form of a conclusion that, in a particular situation, it would be right to do one thing and wrong to do another.

Again, to outsiders, it may appear that, for all the discourse, these ultimate conclusions of right and wrong rest on purely personal, subjective feelings or hunches or instincts or intuitions about right and wrong. When a postconsequentialist discourse leads the discoursers to agree about moral principles, it may be simply because they happened to be a set of persons who already had roughly the same personal moralities before the discourse began. The discoursers claim otherwise. They believe that they have arrived at statements of moral truth that are more objective than a mere collective statement of their individual moral preferences.

If the claims of the postconsequentialists are correct, it would follow that there could be public values that were not simply the greatest value preferences of the greatest number. Such values might take the form of overarching general rules that particular public policies would have to obey in order to be legitimate. They might take the form of individual moral rights that no public policy might legitimately impinge. They might enter in the form of a judgment that in a particular situation, a particular public policy was not merely effective or expedient, or the product of group struggle, or capable of yielding the greatest good for the greatest number, but was right or wrong.

What procedures would we use for arriving at such public values and injecting them as governing elements in public policy making? The key to understanding the most recent tendencies of thought about administrative procedure is to be found in observing the tension between the way postconsequentialists do moral philosophy and the demand for wide public participation that marks democratic political theory.

Those who believe that there are statements of right and wrong that go beyond mere personal preference must, of course, have some method or procedure of arriving at such statements. In theory, perhaps, the method might be purely personal and introspective. The individual moral philosopher could work out his or her own rights and wrongs through employing his or her own rational faculties and consulting his or her own moral sentiments or conscience. A number of explanations might be offered for the preference of many contemporary moral philosophers for discourse among a number of persons, rather than introspection, as the best procedure for arriving at truer statements of right and wrong.

The simplest explanation may be that discourse is a very convenient tool for those postconsequentialists who are trying to avoid the label "intuitionist." After all, these moralists are attempting to base the truth of values on appeals to conscience rather than logical demonstration or empirical psychology. They seek to arrive at true, or at least truer, statements of right and wrong through a method that ultimately appeals to what, upon careful moral reflection, seems more true or right or just, or to our moral sense. Such persons are bound to be accused of grounding their moral philosophy in nothing more than their own intuitions or hunches of right and wrong. Intuitionism, of course, comes perilously close to values as mere personal preferences. For isn't an individual very likely to simply stick the label "moral intuition" on whatever he or she prefers? Discourse among a number of persons provides a fairly persuasive makeweight against charges of intuitionism because the discoursers are in a position to challenge one another's appeals to basic moral sense. Such challenges will allow the members of the discoursing group to point out elements of mere personal preference or idiosyncratic moral intuition to one another. Eventually, they can arrive at moral propositions that remain grounded in the moral sense of the individuals in the discoursing group but have been purged of purely personal or intuitionist elements. By exposing personal moral statements to a group process that carefully works out implications, discourse seizes upon inconsistencies and logical flaw. It clarifies ambiguities in the language in which the propositions are stated. It tests one person's initial moral commitments against those of others equally morally sensitive. Moral discourse promises the production of moral values or truths that are far more persuasive than those arrived at by mere individual thought and assertion.

Discourse may also provide a defense against the accusation of Bernard Williams and others that even postconsequentialists fail to take into sufficient account the degree to which any particular moral decision, and especially a decision of public policy, must be unique to the particular and complex web of facts and values implicated in each such decision.[9] Through discourse, the participants in such decisions may be forcibly reminded to explore fully the particular situation before them.

The postpluralists were shopping for some procedure for policy-making to replace, or at least supplement, group struggle. This shopping for new procedures was in part motivated by the perception that groups were rarely sufficiently equal to make the outcome of the struggle fair even in group terms. Remember, however, that it also was motivated by a growing belief that substantive standards of right and wrong, good and bad, public interest and nonpublic interest, ought to be applied to public policies. If the postpluralists were in reality a wing of the movement toward deontological and/or teleological ethics, then perhaps the postpluralists might wish to adopt the same procedure for public policy-making that the philosophers were employing to develop their postconsequentialist ethics, namely discourse. It is at this point that the egalitarian-majoritarian aspects of democratic political theory became a problem. In a democracy, political or public policy decisions ought to be made in a democratic way. As practiced by moral philosophers, discourse appears to be a highly elitist enterprise—the very antithesis of democracy. Such a careful and critical discussion with so much give-and-take can only be undertaken by a small group of persons. Large masses of people can hardly engage in careful conversation each with every other. One of the most important characteristics of ethical discourse, indeed of all modern philosophy, is the careful use of language so as to reduce ambiguity. Few nonphilosophers have the training or the patience to speak so clearly. The philosophers' hypersensitivity to the ambiguity of language has created a style of contemporary ethical discourse that most people would find incredibly boring and tendentious. Each sentence makes sense, but, after a few pages, the lay mind boggles at the seemingly endless flow of distinctions, qualifications and carefully stated assumptions. The "people" or the "voters" can hardly be expected to become ethical discoursers in the style of the philosophers. It is not that postconsequentialist philosophers are asserting that the nation should be run by philosopher-kings. Neither they nor anyone else, however, could expect the vast majority of Americans to do much discourse or the vast majority of public decisions to be arrived at by discourse of this sort.

For those who believe that public policy decisions should be right, rather than merely the product of group struggle, how is the kind of discourse necessary to arrive at right decisions to be introduced into democratic public policy-making? A number of schools of thought are now emerging on this subject. One is that of legal proceduralists.[10] Lawyers, particularly constitutional lawyers, are always looking for special defenses of judicial policy-making. Such defenses are necessary precisely because public policy-making by nonelected, "independent" judges always appears to be antidemocratic. One such defense runs as follows.

Particularly in the appeal of cases with major public policy implications, the litigational process consists of a very careful dialogue between two persons highly trained in a particular mode of discourse. That dialogue between opposing counsel is constrained by a set of legal rules and professional traditions. It is aimed at persuading a set of third persons, the judges. The judges are trained in the same mode of discourse. They are anxious to reach public policy decisions that are justifiable in terms of neutral principles of law which are themselves the product of this same mode of discourse. Molière's "would-be gentleman" was astounded at the discovery that he had been speaking "prose" all along when he thought he had just been speaking. These lawyers discover that litigating lawyers and judges all along have been engaging in the ethical discourse prescribed by the philosophers when what they had thought they were doing was trying a law suit. The continuous stream of constitutional and other policy-laden litigation in the United States can be seen as a continuous discourse about public values engaged in by the set of people best trained in discourse about public values, those who have graduated from the best law schools. The public-value conclusions from this discourse are to be drawn by neutral, principled, independent judges who themselves are, of course, lawyers from the same law schools.

Not all of us are equally charmed by the discovery that a set of Ivy League lawyers are the ideal medium for introducing ethical discourse into public affairs and creating and enforcing our public values. Nor are all of us equally charmed that courts, as opposed to legislatures, or executives, or political parties, or voters are to be the seat of the principles of right and wrong that are to replace group struggle as the criteria for public policy. Yet the alliance between postconsequentialist ethics and the "jurisprudence of values" is becoming an increasingly powerful and persuasive one. It sees judicial processes as a, or even *the*, principal mode of arriving at public values which will then be used by judges to uphold good public policies and strike down bad ones. We shall return to it again and again.

It was relatively easy for lawyers to identify litigation, that is legal discourse, with contemporary ethical discourse. Both modes of discourse are practiced by a few highly trained talkers in sheltered places under a shared set of professional rules and traditions. Litigation is, of course, one of the processes by which public policy is made. So, at least in the minds of the legal proceduralists, litigation becomes a superior mode of insuring correct public policy—that is, policy in accord with deontological standards of the good or policy that contributes to the achievement of public values or the public interest. Through litigation, values are both discovered and enforced upon public policy.

Judicial policy-making has always been of doubtful democratic legitimacy because it is policy-making by a small number of persons not subject to normal, democratic electoral processes. One of the most interesting features of the proceduralists' position is that they compound the elitism of judicial policy-making as a means of increasing its democratic legitimacy. To the elitism of judicial policy-making itself is added the elitism of a few highly trained lawyers discovering and enforcing public values through litigation. This second elitism supposedly cures the first. Judicial policy-making becomes democratic because now it is the way in which public values come to direct public policy.

Yet public values in this sense are not values declared by the public but values declared by the lawyers. Simply attaching the word public to the values discovered in litigation is not enough to make them democratic values. The legal proceduralists offer two responses. The first is that in a legal system where every individual and interest has access to the courts, litigation insures that the values that emerge from it are not idiosyncratic to a single individual or cult, but indwell in the whole society. Second, the very nature of the discourse of litigation leads to true statements of right and wrong, and surely the demos—the people—will accept such true values once they are discovered. The true values discovered by lawyers will become genuine public values, that is, values held by the public. Putting the two together, litigation is a process through which lawyers draw the best ethical propositions out of the moral sentiments of the people, present them to the people for their more specific affirmation and enforce them on the policy-making process when it strays from them under the pressure of more immediate selfish interests. Thus, somewhat magically, we may have both democracy and the enforcement of the values of a small lawyer elite on government policy-making.

We shall return later to this legal proceduralist vision, but most public policy is not made through litigation. Most of it is made through the legislative and administrative processes. We will focus on the administrative process. How can the method of ethical moral discourse be introduced into the administrative process? The major symptom of this effort is the increasing fashionableness of using the word *deliberation* in conjunction with prescriptions for and descriptions of the administrative process.[11] For those who want administrative decisions to be right, rather than merely the product of group struggle, there is increasing interest in administrative deliberation and the use of judicial review to require administrators to deliberate.

It is not entirely clear exactly what administrative deliberation would look like. Some main outlines and some big do's and don'ts are discernable. The administrator is neither to be captured by a particular interest nor to be a mere neutral aggregator of the preferences of the various groups that vie for the agencies' favors. Instead, administrators must seek for and arrive at good public policies, that is, policies that are in accord with deontological standards of right and wrong and/or serve the public interest.

Of course, there have always been notorious difficulties with defining the public interest, but those favoring administrative deliberation seem to mix and match a number of approaches. Some public policy areas involve nothing more than government distribution of a relatively scarce resource on which no one has any particular moral claim, for example, campsites in Yellowstone Park in the summer. In such policy areas, the public interest may be the utilitarian greatest good for the greatest number. Few public policy areas are purely distributive in this sense. In most areas, the proponents of administrative deliberation appear to mean by public interest something like Rousseau's General Will as opposed to the will of all. Administrators should adopt those policies which a fully informed and attentive public itself would have adopted after engaging in serious public debate. Or alternatively, administrators ought to discover true values, either deontological or teleological or both, and apply them to a fully developed understanding of the facts so as to arrive at correct public policies. Such policies would, of course, be in the public interest both in the sense of achieving the general good and in the sense of meriting public approval, for surely the people would approve the good either tacitly or actively once it was pointed out to them.

The jurisprudence of values has focused on judges, and particularly on judges in constitutional interpretation. In part because of our fascination with the common law, and in part because of our constitutional traditions, it does not seem at all strange to us to conceive of judges as "discovering" values or principles and serving as moral leaders. It is easy to suppose certain values potentially available in the common law or the Constitution which the judges slowly make explicit and bring to the fore through litigation-based legal discourse. It is even easy to suppose that the judges are not themselves creating the values and the policies that flow from them but only leading the people to explicitly acknowledge values which have long been moving toward fruition in the people's own moral consciousness.

Such a jurisprudence deliberately conflates two sources of values in order to overcome democratic difficulties. The first source is pie in the sky. The judges say, "We got our values from the eternal principle of the common law" or, "We got our values from the Constitution." It turns out, however, that there is no authoritative source for the moral meaning of the common law or the Constitution other than the judges themselves. The second source is an imaginary people. The judges say, "We are only making explicit values that were already developing in the public or the society or the people." It turns out, however, that the judges are quite prepared to announce and stick to these values even when a majority of the people profess to reject them or there is no clear evidence that the judicially-announced value is any more endemic to the society than any number of rival values.

If the jurisprudence of values has difficulties with its democratic critics even when it is applied to the value work of common law and constitutional judges, how much rockier is the path when it is applied to administrators. Administrators do not hold lawyers' seances with the common law. They are not lawyers trained in those sacred mysteries. Nor can they claim that direct line to the constitutional gods claimed by the Supreme Court. From whence and how are mere administrators to derive their values?

One answer is that they are to derive them just as judges do, through a process of litigation that serves as the equivalent of the moral discourse conducted by philosophers. As we shall see later, there has been an increasing tendency toward turning administrative decision making into a quasi-judicial process in which policy emerges from trial-like administrative hearings. The administrators become lawyer-like moral discoursers.

A second answer is simply that administrative deliberation ought to be like philosophic discourse. *Deliberation* comes to signify a process in which administrators seek to identify the public interest or common good by engaging in discourse among themselves and with relevant groups. That discourse is to be explicitly aimed at arriving at deontological and or teleological statements of basic values that serve as guides to policy outcomes. The administrators become moral philosophers.

A third answer is that administrators are not free moral actors. They administer, that is implement or carry out, statutes. Statutes prescribe the organization and duties of administrative agencies. They create the programs that the administrators are to carry out. Therefore those administering a program ought to adopt the values and goals that the legislature puts into the statute creating it. Administrative deliberation becomes a process of statutory interpretation. The administrator seeks to discover the true values in the statute, a task that is not as easy as it sounds for reasons we will get to shortly.

So far we have seen a negative and a positive side to administrative deliberation. It is not to be a process of simply aggregating group demands. It is to be a process of identifying the public interest or common good or basic values that will then guide actual policy outcomes. Something else is also involved. For both utilitarians and postconsequentialists, a correct public policy decision rests not only on a correct set of values, but on an accurate assessment of facts. This point is most easily understood by a brief digression into theories of decision making.

For some years those interested in the decision-making process in complex organizations have distinguished between two styles of decision making which are often called *synoptic* and *incremental*.[12] Synoptic means seeing everything. A synoptic decision maker identifies and assigns relative priorities to all relevant values, learns all the facts of the real world and canvasses every possible alternative policy. The synoptic decision maker then chooses that policy alternative that is most likely to achieve the highest levels of the appropriate values at the least cost. That choice is right. For example, if international peace is the prime value to be served, and national security the next most important, the defense policymaker simply learns all the facts about all the nations of the world and their intentions. He considers every conceivable mix of armaments from star wars to unilateral disarmament. He then chooses precisely that weapons posture for the United States that is most likely to lead to world peace at the least risk to our security and the least strain to our economy.

As the example suggests, the critics of synopticism argue that it is neither an accurate description of how decisions are made in the real world nor a rational theory of decision making. The basic problem with synopticism is that it fails to take into account the costs of making decisions. For instance if an organization could not make a decision until it knew all the relevant facts, it might have to spend billions of dollars in order to gather all the facts. Indeed it would often be forbidden to make any decision because often there is simply no way of knowing all the facts. No one in his right mind would try to know every fact there is to know about home computers before deciding which one to buy. Some of the facts, like what new improvements will be made three years from now, we cannot really know at all.

Critics of synopticism offer an alternative theory, called incrementalism, which takes account of the costs of decision making. Incrementalists argue that real organizations actually make decisions without fully stating and agreeing on priorities for their values. They do not make a decision at all until something appears to be so wrong with their current policy that they are forced to change. In other words, they do not first decide what it would be right to do and then do it. Instead, they keep doing what they are doing until they see that what they are doing is very wrong. Then they decide to move away from the wrong, rather than deciding to move toward a clearly defined right. It is far easier for human beings to agree that X is wrong and we ought to do something else than it is to agree on exactly what is right.

In moving away from the wrong, decision makers will consider only a few alternatives to what they are doing now. They will learn only a limited number of new facts that seem particularly important to the few new alternatives they are considering. To consider all alternatives and gather all facts would cost too much time and money. The new alternatives considered will be ones close to the policy now in force. It is too hard to think up radically different ways of doing things and to predict the consequences of radical change. If we are used to wooden tennis rackets with gut strings, we may think about aluminum rackets with nylon strings. It will take us a long time before we begin thinking about giving up the racket all together and substituting an electronically generated magnetic field that repels an electrically charged tennis ball made of zinc. Because it is too hard, too costly, and just plain impossible to get all our values straight, consider all alternatives, and learn all the facts, organizations tend to make new decisions by small steps or increments. Each new policy adopted is only a little different from the old policy and builds on it.

The final advantage of this incremental decision process has to do with the costs of error. Every human decision runs the risk

of being wrong. If we make big new radically different decisions, we run the risk of being very, very wrong and not knowing we are wrong until it is too late. If we decide on a new policy
that we hope is a little righter than the current one, it may turn
out to be a little righter. At worst, however, it will probably not
turn out to be much wronger. Whatever unanticipated costs or
wrongs the new policy creates will probably be small ones and
relatively easily corrected. By taking small steps and then eval-
uating the new information we get from those steps, we can
gradually improve our policies without running big risks. Before
diving into the lake, it is best to stick a toe in to find out the
temperature, and then wade in to find out the depth. Those
who jump in risk freezing and a broken neck. Small step
changes, followed by feedback, and then more small changes
based on that feedback, greatly reduce the risk of trying new
things.

Incrementalism had obvious attractions for pluralists and
those who believe that right and wrong were simply statements
of individual and group preference. Administrators reacting to
multiple group pressures were hardly likely to make decisions
that met synoptic standards. Instead they were likely to do
nothing until they had to react to some group's demands. Then
they made a series of small, compromise changes in policy until
they reached a policy that satisfied all the groups enough so that
pressure on the agency subsided. Such a process of aggregating
group preferences could now be dignified with the name incrementalism. It could be argued that decisions made by government agencies had to be, and indeed ought to be, incremental.
What looked like haphazard, piecemeal government response to
group pressure without any concern for long-term public interests was instead incrementalism, the only rational decision-
making process for a large organization confronting a complex
world.

In its treatment of values, incrementalism represented the
high point in the morality of personal preference that dominated
philosophy until the recent developments that have been
labeled postconsequentialist. Incrementalism not only treated

all values as mere preferences but even gave up any attempt to build value consensus as a basis for policy making. Incrementalists argued that if people had to wait until they agreed on exactly what they wanted and how much they wanted each thing relative to every other thing they wanted, they would never be able to decide anything. Twelve people trying to decide on whether to go to a Chinese, Italian, French, or Japanese restaurant is a classic example. They would all starve before they worked out exactly which restaurant absolutely best met all their preferences.

Incrementalists argued that, faced with problems such as these, what people did, and what it was rational for them to do, was to arrive at decisions which, in Herbert Simon's expression, *satisficed*.[13] A "satisficing" decision did not satisfy anyone in the sense of giving her exactly what she wanted. Indeed the participants rarely bothered to work out exactly what they wanted. Instead, they would all agree to the first proposed decision that they could all live with or would all like at least a little bit. Each would agree to be "satisficed" instead of satisfied because they all knew that otherwise they would reach no decision at all. As soon as enough interest groups were so unhappy with current government policy that they knew they wanted a change, they would agree to the first change proposed that left them all at least a little better off than they had been before. They did so because each group knew that no change would occur if it held out for what it wanted most. Indeed groups often didn't even bother to decide what they wanted most.

Incrementalism taught that the question, Is this proposed policy good or right? was foolish. Even seeking to discover principles of right and wrong, or common good, or public interest, or visions of the good person in the good state, was self-defeating for administrators charged with policy-making authority. Instead of all this pie in the sky, the administrator should keep quiet until trouble, in the form of group pressure, arose. Then he should start throwing up proposals for small step changes in current policy until he found one that all the groups were prepared to live with. Seeking values to guide policy was not a rational thing to do.

Once the fit between pluralism, morality as preference, and incremental decision theory has been observed, it is easy to see what one of the major elements in postpluralist, postconsequentialist prescriptions for administrative deliberation would have to be. The administrator should engage in synoptic decision making.

The reply to the incrementalist critics of synopticism is that they have exaggerated the demands and costs of synopticism. Of course it is impossible to know everything and consider everything. The question is one of degree. Incrementalism tends to excuse inadequate research and analysis and confused policy goals. Synopticism demands that, within reasonable cost and time constraints, the agencies do, not a perfect, but the best possible job of gathering facts and identifying alternatives. Within the same constraints, they should articulate the values that have led to their choices among alternatives. Of course there are policy areas where crucial facts simply cannot yet be known given the state of scientific knowledge. On these "frontiers of science," even the synopticist must sometimes proceed by best guess. But even then the administrative agency can be called upon to demonstrate that the problem is indeed at the frontiers of science and that it has made the best guess it can rather than the first one that occurred to it.[14] The demand is that administrators do the best possible job, not the least that will "satisfice" the interest groups. We shall see later that courts have increasingly demanded that agencies act synoptically.

The vision of agency deliberation has been built up to oppose the vision of administrators as mere incremental aggregators of group preferences and captives of dominant groups. It is not that groups are to be excluded from the deliberations conducted by administrators. They are to be allowed a voice. Ultimately, however, administrators are to conduct an ethical discourse quite comparable to that conducted by philosophers and judges. The purpose of this discourse is to identify true public values.

Administrators are to add to this discourse a technical expertise that, within reasonable time and cost constraints, allows them to discover all the facts and consider all the alternative policies. Putting values, facts, and alternatives together, they are to arrive at correct public policies—policies that accord with the deontological values of the society and move it toward its vision of the good person in the good state.

There is a sense in which democracy is not at issue. Surely the people want right administrative decisions, so as long as the administrators arrive at policies by careful deliberation, the people will approve their policies. Many of those who espouse administrative deliberation, however, add a series of democratic controls. All interest groups are to have as nearly as possible equal access to the deliberators. There is to be a public record of the deliberation. The deliberators are to provide the public a reasoned explanation of their decision. In their search for values, administrators are to take the values incorporated into the governing statutes by the democratically elected legislature as crucial. Courts will engage in judicial review of administrative decisions to insure that they are in accord with the values and goals of the democratically elected legislature. Administrative deliberation somehow manages to combine ethical discourse, technological expertise and democratic responsiveness.

The key bridge between deliberation and democracy is the notion of a deliberative community which has its origins in the Greek idea of the polis. The polis is the Greek city state in which all the citizens participate in making decisions about all matters of public concern. A central aspect of postconsequential concepts of deliberation is the call for a political community in which all aspects of government, including administration, would be embedded.[15]

To sum up, those in revolt against the pluralist, incrementalist theory of politics and administration did not have to content themselves with negative carping at the unfairness of the group struggle. Instead, they found in postconsequentialist ethical discourse a model for postpluralist administration. Such administration was to combine ethical discourse and technical expertise to achieve synoptic policy decisions that were both intrinsically correct and democratic. Postconsequentialist philosophy and postpluralist political theory are thus central to the current fascination of administrative lawyers and administrative theorists with deliberation.

So far, we have been looking at how very broad movements in moral and political philosophy have been providing a new vision of administration as deliberation. In attempting to describe and account for changes in our ways of thinking about and doing administration and changes in our prescriptions for judicial review of administration, we are dealing with very central and very practical features of American politics. When dealing with central political developments, it is rarely wise to look at them only from the perspective of very broad movements in social thought. Politics is always a matter of ideology as well as philosophy. Great ideas are turned into weapons to serve various political interests and institutions. To understand what is actually happening, it is necessary to track this transmutation of ideas into ideology.

Moreover, our particular political topic, the relation of courts to administrators, is heavily laden with law. It often makes things clearer to treat law as if it developed on its own with some degree of autonomy from both ethical and political theory and political ideology. Accordingly, we are going to go through the story of how current notions of administrative "deliberation" emerged twice more, once in terms of the development of administrative law from the 1930s to the present and then again in terms of changes in political ideology during the same period.

Chapter Two

The Growth of

Administrative Law

The story of the development of American administrative law, that is, the law governing how government agencies administer their programs and courts review them, has been told many times and only a brief summary is necessary here.[1] English and American law, the so-called "common law," initially denied that there was any such thing as administrative law. It made that denial central to the basic liberties of the citizen. As enunciated by the great turn-of-the-century English liberal, Alfred Dicey, the central guarantee of individual freedom was the rule of law. We lived under a government of laws, not men. Government could not act against individuals when it pleased, how it pleased, or for whatever reason it pleased. It could only act according to preexisting general laws passed by a representative legislative body like Parliament or Congress. For Dicey, one of the central features of the rule of law was that, when a dispute arose between government and an individual about whether government had acted according to law, that dispute would be submitted to the regular courts as a normal law suit. The government would be treated as simply one of the parties, granted no more consideration by the judge than any other party. In this way, the rule of law could be enforced on government as it was on individuals, by the courts.

The "Roman" or "civil" law tradition of France and the rest of the continent of Europe had a centuries-old tradition of administrative law. Dicey rejects that tradition precisely because it creates a body of administrative law separate from the general body of law and a separate set of courts to enforce it. Dicey argues that only by submitting government to the ordinary law in the ordinary courts, by treating government as if it were legally only an individual like other individuals, can we insure that government is not given special legal privileges that would allow it to escape from subordination to the rule of law.[2]

What condemned continental administrative law in the eyes of English liberals was that it did provide a special status for the state. In European administrative law, the state was viewed as the guardian of the public interest. Administrative law judges necessarily inclined toward its position over that of the purely private interests of the individual challenging the state's action, unless the state had clearly acted unlawfully. Thus, long before the dominance of the American pluralist political theory of the 1950s, the terms of the basic debate were set. Dicey and company saw only a multitude of interests. Where government was involved, its interest was to be treated just like any other, as a particular preference to be balanced against the preference of the individual with whom the state had come into conflict. Proponents of a special administrative law, on the other hand, saw the government as bound to serve the public interest or the common good. The purpose of administrative law was to insure that government officials were meeting their obligation to serve the public.

Dicey's position toward administrative law dominated American legal thinking in the early part of the twentieth century. That dominance had a number of very important consequences. Because they had begun by denying that administrative law existed or ought to exist, when Americans finally started to invent such a law, it had a kind of catch-up, piecemeal quality. We create administrative law a little bit at a time, each bit reacting to changes in actual administrative practice or changes in our broader political ideas. Because we did not begin with a tradition of special administrative courts, we have continually debated the role of our regular courts in supervising administration. Finally, we have continued to be uncertain about whether and how a concept of government as representative of the public interest ought to be introduced into our administrative law.

Beginning with the creation of the Interstate Commerce Commission in 1888, the administrative apparatus and practices of the United States began to change and expand far beyond the rudimentary cabinet departments that had existed earlier. It was the sudden, enormous, and politically controversial expansion of the federal bureaucracy by the New Deal, however, that led to a crucial reevaluation of the Diceyan tradition that had dominated American legal thought. The New Deal itself was full of lawyers. The last thing it wanted was lawless administration. The opponents of the New Deal, however, were vigorously reasserting the Diceyan position. The regular courts were imbued with traditional legal respect for private property and staffed by Republican judges appointed in the 1920s. They would protect the business community and the individual from the outburst of New Deal intervention in what had previously been considered private economic relationships. If disputes between government regulators and those they regulated could be brought into regular courts, where the government would be treated as just another litigant, then this kind of judicial protection of private interests would be most likely to occur.

This debate was conducted within the traditional categories of nineteenth-century liberal political theory and utilitarianism. The enemies of the New Deal argued that individual rights must be protected from the overweening power of the state. The New Deal argued that government agencies must be left free to serve the greatest good of the greatest number or the public interest so long as they did not act arbitrarily or unlawfully.

In the period just before World War II, the New Deal staved off conservative attempts to get a major new administrative law statute through Congress. Such a statute might have subjected government agencies to extremely demanding court-enforced rules protecting the individual interests of those regulated by government. The New Deal managed to prevent such a statute, however, only by establishing a presidential commission to conduct its own elaborate investigation of agency practices and issue its own procedural guidelines. The success in keeping Congress out and insuring that administrative law would be of the executive branch, by the executive branch, and for the executive branch was short-lived. In 1946, Congress passed a major administrative procedures act.

Nevertheless, one of the great and lasting success of the New Deal was to establish more firmly than ever the catch-up and piecemeal quality of American administrative law. The president's commission called the Attorney General's Committee on Administrative Procedure issued a major report in 1941. It was able to .establish a basic methodological principle for making administrative law. The principle was that because the actual practices of government agencies were necessarily so many, so complex and so varied, they could not be governed by a single, simple set of uniform rules. Whatever rules were made had to be derived pragmatically from existing agency practice. In short, new administrative law was to legitimate what the New Deal was doing, not dictate rules to it that would hinder its activities.[3]

The Administrative Procedures Act (APA) of 1946 adopted precisely this principle. It was not an administrative code, that is, a basic and complete set of legal rules governing all administrative action. Instead, it was a residual and back-up statute. Where the particular statute creating a government agency or a specific government program did not specify how the agency was to do certain things, then the agency was to look to the general provisions of the APA. To this day, when a lawyer wants to know what rules an agency must follow, he first looks at the statute setting up the agency and any subsequent amendments to it. Then he looks at the statute setting up the particular program, such as inspecting citrus fruit or loaning money to small business, that the agency is running. Then he refers to the APA. The administrative law of the United States remains scattered through hundreds of statutes.

The APA is not only incomplete and residual. Just as the New Dealers wanted it to, it also basically reflects the ways the agencies had already been acting. Mostly, it simply writes existing practices into law. This does not mean that it totally deprived individuals of rights or vested unlimited power in administrators. As we have already seen, the New Deal was full of lawyers.

They had built many procedural and substantive protections for individuals into the New Deal statutes of the 1930s which set up such new agencies as the Securities and Exchange Commission and the National Labor Relations Board. And the New Deal lawyers who staffed the agencies had insisted that the agencies create and follow decent procedural rules. Nevertheless, agency practice tended to be far more oriented to government action "in the public interest" and less to protection of individual interests than the conservative critics of the New Deal would have wanted. This balance was preserved by the APA.

At the heart of the APA is a grand compromise between the Diceyan view and the New Deal view. Many regulatory statutes required that an agency hold hearings before taking action that directly affected the interests of some particular individual or firm adversely. By 1946, hearing practices were well established in many agencies. The Diceyan view that all disputes between individuals and government should be tried in the regular courts had already been defeated by events. Administrative agencies were already holding hundreds of trial-like proceedings each year on their own. One of their own employees acted as a sort of "trial judge." The heads of the agencies acted like appeals courts reviewing the outcome of the proceedings. The APA approves this widespread practice of administrative adjudication conducted within the agencies rather than in the regular courts, and conducted under special administrative procedures rather than the legal procedures of the regular courts. It firmly rejects the view that there should be no administrative law at all—that all disputes between government and individuals should go to the regular courts under regular law.

On the other hand, the APA requires that such administrative adjudications be conducted almost as if they were trials. The private party involved may be represented by counsel, may offer both oral and written testimony, and may cross examine. The proceedings must be presided over by a "hearing officer" who, although an employee of the agency, must not have had anything to do with the decision of the agency to bring the proceeding against the individual. (Later amendments to the APA have changed the title to "administrative law judge" and required that such judges be almost entirely independent of agency control.) The agency's decision or holding must be in writing and be supported by findings based on substantial evidence in the record as a whole, and agency holdings in administrative adjudications, with very few exceptions, are to be reviewable by the regular federal courts. Thus the APA legitimates agency adjudications, but requires them to be very much like trials in regular courts and ultimately to be supervised by the regular courts.

Remember that the APA is a catch-up statute trying to provide law to cover legitimate agency practices that were already growing up. By 1946, agencies and courts had done a lot of adjudication about matters in which the government was in conflict with some outside party. Reflecting this wealth of familiar experience, the APA could be and was very explicit and detailed. It was easy for a statute to say how adjudications should be conducted because both courts and agencies already had plenty of rules for conducting then. The APA essentially says to the agencies, "Where a statute authorizes you to do so, you may conduct an adjudication. When you conduct an adjudication, conduct it as a court does. And an appeals court, which is used to reviewing trial court adjudications, will review yours."

Rule Making

In 1946, however, far less was known about how to conduct another kind of agency legal activity that agencies had always done, but that had taken an enormous spurt in the New Deal. This other kind of activity was rule making. Statutes passed by legislative bodies rarely are detailed enough to cover every aspect of every possible situation. Suppose Congress passes a statute that reads, "No vehicles may be operated in an officially designated wilderness area." Now suppose someone rides a horse into a wilderness area. Has she violated the statute? Probably not. We would not suppose that when Congress said no vehicles, it meant no horses. Now suppose someone drives a sled into a snowy wilderness. The sled is powered by a motor-driven propellor. Probably Congress hadn't been thinking about propellor-driven sleds when it said *vehicle*, but we probably would conclude that such a sled was a vehicle within the meaning of the statute. Now how about a horse-drawn sled? Does the statute prohibit horse-drawn sleds in wilderness areas? Precisely because Congress knows that problems like these are bound to arise, it often includes in statutes like this one a provision that authorizes the agency involved to make rules.

In this instance the Department of the Interior, which administers wilderness areas, might have the power to make a rule that horse-drawn sleds are allowed in wilderness areas but propellor-driven sleds are not. Such rules are sometimes called sublegislation or delegated legislation. Congress could have written a provision into its statutes about sleds. Or, once the sled problem became apparent, Congress could have passed a sled amendment to its statute. Another thing Congress can do, however, is delegate a part of its own power to make law about vehicles in wildernesses to the agency that the statute authorizes to administer the wildernesses. In effect Congress says "We make the general law—no vehicles. We give some of our power to make laws to the Department of the Interior so that they can make the more detailed rules necessary to carry out the general rule we have made." Agency rules get their authority from this delegation of law-making power by Congress. The detailed rules the agencies make must be in harmony with the general rule announced in the congressional statute.

As our example shows, the agencies have some power to choose among various policies. An agency might argue, for instance, that it seemed to it that the purpose of the wilderness statute was to preserve large areas for the few people willing to take the time and energy to walk in. So it might make a rule that even horses were vehicles prohibited by the statute. Or it might say that even if horses were not vehicles, horse-drawn sleds were. If they were not considered prohibited vehicles, too many people would get into the wilderness with too little of their own effort. Or the agency might make a rule allowing horse-drawn but not propellor-driven sleds on the basis that a wilderness ought to be a quiet place. Motor sleds make too much noise and horse-drawn sleds almost none. Rule making is law making.

In making rules, agencies choose among policy alternatives. Rule making is subordinate law making. The commanding congressional statute forbids the agency to choose some alternatives and requires it to choose others. Under the no-vehicle law, the agency has no choice but to make a rule banning pickup trucks and could not make a rule banning hikers. But it can certainly choose either to ban or not to ban horse-drawn sleds.

Agencies had been delegated some rule-making powers by Congress from the earliest days of the Republic. During the New Deal, however, the amount of this delegation increased enormously and often the statute placed almost no limits on the agencies' choices. A few simply said that, within the programs it administered, an agency could make any rules it wanted so long as they served "the public interest."

Nor did the New Deal statutes establish many rule-making procedures. The Constitution and Congress's own rules set up rather elaborate procedures for law making by Congress. Most of us learned in high school civics the elaborate set of steps by which a bill is introduced, first in one house of Congress and then in the other, moves through committees to floor debate and votes in each house, and then to a conference committee, and finally on to presidential signature or veto. Most of the laws delegating rule-making power to agencies did not, however, specify what procedures agencies were to use in making rules. By 1946, the agencies had not settled down to any very fixed set of practices for making rules, as they had for agency adjudications. There was no average, common, or usual way to make rules shared by a lot of agencies. So the APA could not write existing agency rule-making practice into new statutory law as it had agency adjudicative practice.

Yet there was a lot of rule making. The APA couldn't just ignore it. Consequently the APA has a rule-making section but a very sketchy one. It requires that the agency give notice that it is contemplating a rule, receive comments from interested outsiders, print its final rule in the *Federal Register* and accompany the published rule with a concise and general statement of its basis and purpose. Reflecting these provisions, we speak of "notice and comment" rule making or "informal" rule making because these rules are made by informal rather than formal, trial-like procedures. The APA provides that such rules are reviewable by the United States Courts of Appeal. The courts are to strike down rules that are unlawful, arbitrary and capricious, or an abuse of discretion. Most of the development of administrative law in the sixties and seventies that we are going to look at was an attempt to flesh out these few sketchy rule-making provisions of the APA.

Administrative agencies make thousands of decisions of a wide variety of kinds that are neither administrative adjudication nor rule making. For instance, the Department of Transportation must approve local plans on where to route interstate highways. The Department of Interior must grant permits to ranchers to graze cattle on publicly owned range land. The APA did not attempt to categorize or subdivide this mass of decision making or to specify rules for it. It only provided that all such decisions were subject to judicial review for "abuse of discretion." We still tend to lump all these decisions together under the catchall category "discretion" or sometimes "informal adjudication," although many of them do not involve adjudicating a conflict between disputants. While we will concentrate on rule making, many of the same problems about judicial control of agency action arise in roughly the same way in the area of discretion.[4]

The New Administrative Law: Stage One, Pluralism

Let us turn to post-1946 catch-up developments in the administrative law of how to do administrative rule making. To do so, we must remind ourselves of how the history of political and moral philosophy and the history of administrative law overlap. We have seen that the first stage of American administrative law, which was the fight over whether to have such a law at all, was greatly influenced by the late-nineteenth-century liberal political theory of individual rights against the state. In its adjudication provisions, the APA still reflects that individualist theory. Before an administrative agency may infringe on what might be a legal right of an individual, it must conduct a hearing which is very like a trial. That trial must be reviewable by a regular federal court. As written, the rule-making provisions of the APA are not oriented to any particular political theory except two fundamental notions derived from older rule of law and democratic thought: government must make all of its rules public so that people cannot be punished for violating rules they could not have known existed; people should have a chance to say what kind of law they want before it is made.

In the sixties and seventies the then-dominant theory of pluralism was poured into the nearly empty rule-making provisions of the APA. Remember that the essential vision of pluralism was that interest groups, not individuals, were the basic units of politics. Democracy demanded that all groups have easy access to government decision makers. In administrative law, the two key sets of government decision makers are the agencies and the courts that review their decisions. The first step in pluralizing rule making was to expand what lawyers call "standing," that is the legal right to appear before an agency or court. By court decisions interpreting the APA and other statutes, and by new congressional legislation, more and more groups were given the right to participate in agency rule-making proceedings and to file law suits in court challenging agency rules they didn't like. Originally, only those who had a preexisting legal right that was infringed upon by a rule could challenge that rule in court. Eventually, anyone who was "arguably within the zone of interests" protected by a statute and had suffered even the slightest injury in fact was granted standing.

One of the most famous cases involved a rail freight rate for shipping scrap metal approved by the Interstate Commerce Commission, which at the time set freight rates.[5] Originally only the railroads involved and perhaps the shippers of scrap would have had standing to challenge the rate. In the *Scrap* case, a group of persons argued that if the scrap rate were set too high, scrap yards wouldn't ship as much scrap, and if they didn't ship as much, they wouldn't buy as much, and if they didn't buy as much, less scrap would be collected from along roadsides and from woods and fields, and if less were collected, there would be more litter, and if there were more litter, the aesthetic pleasure that members of the group got from roaming through the countryside would be reduced. This group was granted standing to challenge the rail rate.

Expanding standing was one step in increasing group access to government. Pluralism taught that such access was meaningless, however, unless government actually listened to what the groups had to say and then did what they wanted. Every aspect of the APA requirements for rule making was used to increase the meaningfulness of such group access.

The principal mode of group access provided by the APA for rule making was, of course, the provision that required the rule-making agencies to accept comments on proposed rules from the interested public. Unless the groups had some idea of what rule the agency had in mind, however, it was very hard to prepare such comments. The Department of Interior might give notice that it was drafting a vehicles-in-the-wilderness rule. A group might devote its whole comment to explaining why the agency should not adopt a rule banning horses only to discover too late that the agency itself was interested only in a possible ban on snow mobiles. Much court and congressional action went into expanding notice requirements so that the agency had to indicate what data it had, how it had analyzed the data and what alternatives it was considering. In this way groups were assisted in making more pointed and effective comments.

Even very pointed and relevant comments don't provide meaningful access to a group if the agency involved ignores the comments. Courts that reviewed agency action, and most particularly the Court of Appeals for the District of Columbia, or D.C. Circuit as it is usually called, began to insist that agencies listen.

But how can a reviewing court be sure that an agency has actually paid attention to a comment submitted to it in writing or even to an oral presentation?

At trials, judges must listen carefully to both sides. They do so in part because they feel it is their duty as judges, but also because judges know nothing about the matter before them and can only find out by listening. An agency that contemplates a rule about chickens is likely to have on its own staff a dozen people with advanced degrees in poultry science who have devoted their lives to the study of chickens. The chicken agency will have conducted its own studies that have collected hundreds of thousands of pages of data about chickens. The agency will have considered many alternative policies and run pilot or test programs. It is likely to feel it already has its values straight, with the good health of chickens high on its list of value priorities. By the time it gives notice of a proposed rule, it may well feel that it knows everything there is to know about chickens and certainly far more than any outside group could know. Furthermore, it feels that its knowledge and analysis are objective and unbiased, unlike that of the outside groups like growers and packers and supermarkets and consumers, each of whom has its own axe to grind. The result may be that the agency really does not want to waste time going over the reams of material submitted by interest groups. The agency may feel such material will only contain partisan distortions of information it already has considered.

Reviewing courts, therefore, shopped for special ways to enforce their pluralistic requirement that the agencies give all groups meaningful access to the decision-making process. They arrived at a solution that came to be called the "dialogue" requirement. One way to insure that someone has really listened is to require that he respond to everything that is said to him. He must listen in order to respond even if he doesn't believe it is worth listening because he knows everything already. The courts came to say that a rule maker had to respond to every significant comment submitted to the agency. One way the agencies made a record of their responses was to expand the concise and general statement that the APA required accompany each rule. These statements became anything but concise and general as they became detailed responses to interest group comments.

The most important change in administrative law that occurred because of the dialogue requirement, however, was the invention by the courts of an entirely new procedural requirement for rule making, the requirement of a rule-making record. This requirement is not in the APA. Indeed it would appear to be quite out of kilter with the APA's basic arrangement. We have seen that the APA carved out two basic categories of administrative action, adjudication and rule making. It made administrative adjudication "formal," that is as much like court trials as possible. It made rule making informal, involving only notice, comment, and concise and general statement. At the time the APA was written, nothing was as closely associated with formal trial-type proceedings as a "record," that is a printed compilation of all the oral and written evidence offered. Indeed, for years Congress has conveyed its intention that an agency conduct an adjudication by inserting into the authorizing statute a requirement that the agency make the decision "on the basis of substantial evidence on the record as a whole." One of the main distinctions between an adjudication and a rule making was that an adjudication required a record and a rule making did not.

Yet, beginning in the 1960s, courts increasingly began to refer to something they called a "rule-making record." Congress also began to use this language in some of its new statutes. Eventually courts required a "rule-making record" in rule making just as they required a "record" in adjudication. The rule-making record was a printed record of all the comments plus the agencies' replies to those comments. The courts invented the rule-making record as a way of enforcing the dialogue requirement. With rule-making records in front of them, judges could see whether the agency had replied to each comment and thus whether the agency had really granted meaningful access—had really listened—to every group.[6]

Along with the dialogue requirement, the D.C. Circuit also

announced the "hard look" doctrine.[7] Reviewing courts were to insure that rule-making agencies had taken a hard look at all the evidence. Finally, the courts required that the agencies show that they had reached their final rule by "reasoned decision making." In the pluralist-oriented administrative law of the sixties, dialogue, rule-making record, hard look and reasoned decision making were all woven together to create an administrative procedure that insured that all groups would be heard. Taken together they defined a right decision as any decision that clearly demonstrated that it had taken all interests into account.

The New Administrative Law: Stage Two, Postpluralist Synopticism

At the very time that this pluralist edifice of administrative procedure and judicial review of that procedure was being completed, disillusion with pluralism was already setting in. Perhaps access to agencies could never be sufficiently equalized, given the widely varying resources of various groups. And perhaps there was a public interest or a right public policy quite apart from the sum of group interests.

The first response of administrative law to these doubts about pluralism was an almost frantic pursuit of more and more perfect pluralism. If some groups did not have enough money to compete with others in access to rule makers, then perhaps the rule-making agencies ought to provide public funding to the poorer groups to equalize access. If there was a chance that none of the groups directly affected by a proposed rule or the sum of all such groups adequately represented the public interest, then perhaps standing ought to be expanded to everyone, even to persons who really had no special interest other than that of a good citizen.[8] In this way it could be hoped that at least one person who stood for the right and the good would pop up to sue the agency or otherwise require it to take a hard look at what the interest groups preferred to ignore.

Most importantly, the courts began to pour over the rule-making record. They invalidated rules if they could find even the tiniest mumble by the tiniest group to which the rule-making agency had not responded. In the most famous of these cases a group had listed to an agency dozens of things it wanted the agency to consider. When the agency had asked the group to say something more about each of these things, the group had refused. The D.C. Circuit nonetheless said that the agency had acted improperly in not pursuing the analysis of each and every one of them.[9] In this particular case, the Supreme Court said that the dialogue requirement had been driven too far when it required that an agency respond to a group that in fact had refused to engage in dialogue.[10] The D.C. Circuit responded to the Supreme Court by saying it would keep doing what it had been doing, if necessary by saying that an agency had not engaged in reasoned decision making unless it responded to everything.[11]

As administrative law sought to cure the hiatuses and pathologies of group politics by introducing more group politics in the frenzied search for perfect group politics, something else was happening. By the late 1970s and the early 1980s, administrative law was actually undergoing a conversion from pluralism and consequentialism to postpluralism and postconsequentialism.

We ought not to exaggerate the sharpness of the break with pluralism. Much of the conversion was gradual and unconscious and developed themes already present in the pluralist period. We have already noted, for instance, that not all pluralists had pushed their position on the public interest to the extreme of arguing that there was no public interest aside from the sum of group preferences. Instead, they could argue that the true public interest, whatever it was, could best be achieved if all groups competed before the agencies. This competition would insure that the agency saw all sides and was not captured or excessively influenced by one selfish interest. The group competition could help the expert agency to arrive at the right answer or the true public interest. Pluralists never made very clear whether group politics was a good thing because there were no right answers or because group politics was the best way to arrive at right answers. As the belief grew that there were some right answers or at least some more right answers, it was easy for postconsequentialists to pick up certain pluralist requirements, see them as pluralist *means* to achieving deontological or teleological ends, and insist that it was the ends, not the means, that counted.

This point is most clearly illustrated by the standing and dialogue doctrines that were at the heart of pluralist administrative law. Standing is expanded more and more to give more groups access. But when the final step is taken of giving any individual or group standing, whether or not they are likely to be injured in any way by the proposed rule, is that the ultimate in pluralism? Or is such an ultimate extension based on the idea that there is a real public interest beyond the sum of the group interests. We may want to grant standing, not only to interested groups, but also to disinterested groups and individuals to serve as spokespersons for that public interest. At a certain point the expansion of standing goes beyond improving pluralism with more pluralism and becomes countering pluralism with the intervention of good citizens who will push for the right rather than their own particular interests.

The courts have actually retreated a bit on the standing question in recent years, and Congress has given everyone standing probably in only one statute.[12] It is in the area of dialogue that the greatest shift to postpluralism postconsequentialism has occurred. This shift in legal doctrine has been almost invisible because it has occurred through the omission of a few words from existing doctrinal language rather than through the addition of many new words. Remember that the purpose of the pluralist dialogue requirement was to force the agencies to prove that they had listened to all the groups, thus assuring equality of group access. So the dialogue formula was that in order to prove that they had listened to all groups, agencies must respond to all significant issues *raised by all groups*. What happens, however, if courts begin, as they did begin in the late seventies, to leave out the italicized words and simply say that agencies must respond to all significant issues. Dropping the few words did not seem like such a big break, particularly when the courts had all along been telling the agencies to take a "hard look" and arrive at "reasoned" decisions. Telling the agencies simply to consider all significant issues was a very big break, however, one that we can see clearly if we go back to incremental versus synoptic decision theories.

Remember that incrementalism is closely tied to pluralism and an ethics of personal preference. Its goal is to "satisfice" contending groups without arriving at agreement about values or even conducting a complete analysis of facts and alternative policies. Synopticism demands that values be fully articulated and used as a guide to arriving at a correct policy outcome based on thorough empirical as well as normative analysis. Synopticism is designed to achieve, not a compromise of competing interests, but right answers—right in terms of some agreed and overarching vision of the good. If we discovered administrative law moving from incremental to synoptic demands on agency rule-making processes, we would also be discovering a move from pluralism and the morality of preference to postpluralism and postconsequentialism.

When a court says to an agency, not "Consider all significant issues raised by the parties," but "Consider all significant issues," it has made exactly that shift from pluralism to postpluralism. It no longer says, "Listen to everybody in order to 'satisfice' them." It now says, "Do a synoptic job. Think of everything"—"everything" bounded at the edges by rational cost constraints that tell us not to look at the insignificant. By the late 1970s courts were increasingly demanding that rule making be synoptic.[13]

There are, of course, instances in which rule making cannot be completely synoptic because relevant facts cannot be known with sufficient certainty even to be trusted as mathematically expressed probabilities—instances in which we cannot even say there is about a 30 percent or 40 percent chance that something will happen or that something exists. For these situations courts grant a "frontiers of science" exception to their demand for synopticism. *If* the agency can provide a court with sufficient evidence that it faces a situation in which synopticism is impossible, it will be allowed by the judges to make its best guess. But the reviewing courts are the ultimate judges of when agency synopticism is required and when exemptions are to be granted.

The crucial legal invention that facilitated this judicial move from agency pluralist dialogue to agency synoptic analysis was the rule-making record. When rule-making agencies prepared no record at all, reviewing courts could not possibly know whether the rules they came up with were good or bad. The court saw none of the facts or values on which the rule was based. Indeed, the traditional approach was that courts would presume that agencies had the facts to back their rules while requiring agencies to present a record of the facts to back their adjudicative decisions.

The rule-making record, first invented to enforce pluralist dialogue, willy-nilly became something quite different. Judges demanded that the agencies more and more completely answer in the rule-making record more and more comments made by more and more groups. Courts thus got a more and more complete record of all the facts, values, and alternatives relevant to the particular rule making. When all a court got was a bare notice, the final rule, and a concise and general statement, judges were not much tempted to say whether the rule was right or wrong. They didn't have enough to go on. Once they had a complete rule-making record in front of them, judges were more and more tempted to decide for themselves whether the rule was good or bad.

Initially, the "hard look" doctrine had meant that agencies should take a hard look at the data. It came to have a second meaning as well, that courts should take a hard look at the agencies' decisions. Indeed, the courts announced that they and the agencies were "partners" in taking the hard look. As courts used the rule-making record as a vehicle for demanding synoptic analysis by the agencies, the courts became the senior partners in two senses. First, they had the last word on just how hard a look—just how synoptic—an agency had to be in each particular rule-making proceeding. Second, they ultimately decided not only whether the agency had employed the right rule-making procedures but also whether they had arrived at the substantively correct rule. Synopticism so completely collapses the distinction between using the right decision procedures and reaching the right decision that judicial review to insure that an agency has acted synoptically is necessarily both procedural and substantive review. Courts came to demand routinely that the agencies persuade them that they had made the substantively best policy.[14]

Earlier we noted that incrementalism could serve as an excuse or cover for sloppy and incomplete agency work and for serving special interests instead of seeking the common good or general interest. Incrementalism tended to treat anything that came out of the process of group struggle as, by definition, good. Synopticism demanded substantively right answers arrived at by fully articulating values and analysing facts and alternatives—the right answer by the right analysis. It is little wonder, then, that as suspicion of pluralism grew in American political consciousness, courts began to shift from incrementalism to synopticism as their measure of agency rule-making performance.

We have now tracked two converging and interactive movements that have led us to the notion of agency "deliberation." In the first, changes in our approaches to ethics and political philosophy led to a desire that agency decision makers serve as postconsequentialist public philosophers seeking the public good. In the second, administrative law itself sought to fill out the gigantic hiatus left for rule making in the APA. Initially, it evolved a set of pluralist legal demands. It then gradually shifted to a postpluralist body of law to govern rule making. It really makes very little difference whether or not the judges and legislators who filled out the APA rule-making provisions consciously moved from pluralism to postpluralism and consciously sought to turn administrators into public philosophers engaged in moral discourse. Movements in philosophy and movements in administrative law came together in the vision of the administrator as synoptic seeker of the good.

Chapter Three

Judicial Power

So far, we have been looking at movements in ethics, political theory, and administrative law as changing our thinking about how administrators should act. Actually, however, we have been looking at another phenomenon as well, one of judicial power. Many of the changes in administrative law introduced by courts were echoed and thus legitimated by Congress in new legislation. As we have seen, the APA is not a code. It only comes into play where Congress has not inserted administrative procedure provisions into the statutes creating new agencies and/or new programs. In the sixties and seventies, Congress would often put broad standing provisions, elaborate notice requirements, and rule-making record requirements into the new health, safety, and environmental statutes. In doing so, however, it nearly always was echoing administrative law innovations first imposed by courts on the agencies. How did the courts come to have the power to make such impositions?

Of course, both the American Diceyan tradition and the APA that replaced it gave broad judicial review powers to courts. American courts had always had the power to declare actions of any part of government, including administrative agencies, unconstitutional, but American tradition and the APA also gave the federal courts the additional power to declare administrative actions unlawful. Many administrative actions which did not violate the Constitution, and which agencies could have taken lawfully if they had been authorized by Congress to do so, would be unlawful if not authorized by Congress. Administrative agencies may do lawfully only what congressional statutes authorize them to do. Thus if Congress passed a statute authorizing the Department of Interior to exclude vehicles from wilderness areas, the statute would surely be constitutional and so would an agency rule barring horse-drawn sleds. But if the congressional statute specifically authorized the service to make regulations barring motor-driven vehicles but not horse-drawn ones, then an agency regulation barring horse-drawn sleds would be unlawful. Courts have always had judicial review powers to hear appeals from agency actions and to invalidate unlawful ones.

In the 1960s and 1970s, however, courts began to require many things of the agencies that were not specifically required of them by any congressional statute.[1] The APA itself had imposed only bare notice, comment, and concise and general statement requirements. It also established the standards that courts were to use in reviewing agency action. Following its general plan, the APA imposed a rather strict review standard on adjudication and a very lenient one on rule making. Courts were to review agency adjudications to insure that they were based on substantial evidence on the record as a whole. Courts were to invalidate rule makings, however, only if they were "arbitrary and capricious." There has always been some debate about what those words of the APA mean. Courts initially took them to mean that an agency might make any rule it wished if the agency stuck to the area in which Congress had delegated rule-making power to it, did not violate explicit statutory language, and did not act in a totally unreasonable way. The arbitrary-and-capricious test meant that a court would strike down an agency rule only if no reasonable person could have written such a rule. "Arbitrary and capricious" was a sort of lunacy test.

When we recall that the APA was essentially New Deal legislation that made some compromises with conservative anti-big-government sentiment, we can see why "arbitrary and capricious" was a lunacy test. Liberals and Democrats in general, and the New Deal in particular, had had a lot of trouble with courts in the 1920s and thirties. The Norris-LaGuardia Act of 1932 had barred federal courts from issuing injunctions in labor disputes because the courts had such an anti-union bias. A conservative Supreme Court had used its power of constitutional judicial review to block many of the major New Deal programs. Out of the crisis that resulted came the doctrine of "judi-cial self-restraint" espoused by many liberal lawyers, politicians and judges in the thirties and forties. They argued that most legal questions were really policy questions; so in a democracy like the United States, nonelected courts should defer to the legal decisions of the elected Congress and president.

The very fight over administrative law which culminated in the APA was a fight between conservatives and liberals. Conser-vatives wanted as big a role for the regular courts as possible because they thought of courts as protectors of private property. Liberal New Dealers wanted as small a judicial role as possible because they saw the courts as blocking liberal congressional and especially presidential programs. The APA is, as we have seen, a complex bundle of compromises between the two positions.

Clearly, the conservatives won most on adjudication and least on rule making. For rule making, the conservatives saved judi-cial review by the ordinary courts. The standard of review, how-ever, is clearly an expression of New Deal judicial self-restraint. In a democracy, nonelected federal courts should interfere with policy choices made by the elected president's executive branch, wielding authority given it by an elected Congress, only when the agency's action is very far beyond the law as the Court sees it. Only when an agency rule reflects no conscious policy choice, only when no one could defend it in terms of the policies that Congress and President have announced, in other words only when it is "arbitrary and capricious," should the courts strike it down.

Considered against its New Deal background and in the light of at least the first ten years of actual judicial application of its provisions, the APA gives the federal courts a very, very slight power of judicial review over rule making. Yet, in the 1960s and 1970s, the courts, and particularly the D.C. Circuit, used judicial review to create and impose on the agencies a huge new body of administrative law which was so complex and demanding that it allowed judges to strike down new agency rules whenever they pleased. This new body of law made judges the senior partners to the agencies in taking the "hard look" that would produce reasoned decision making.

In a pinch, the courts still had to use the embarrassing words "arbitrary and capricious," because they were, after all, the words of the APA. But the meaning of the words seemed to change entirely. Instead of the agency being able to have any rule it wanted except crazy ones, the agency now had to produce the best possible rule given all the values, alternatives, and facts involved. Saying you have been arbitrary and capricious if you choose a rule that you cannot convince a court is the best rule is hardly the meaning of "arbitrary and capricious" that the New Dealers had in mind.

So we cannot answer the question, "How did the courts first impose pluralism and then synopticism on the agencies?" simply by saying that American tradition and the APA gave courts the power of judicial review. During the sixties and seventies, the courts redefined and magnified their power of judicial review of agency rule making so greatly as to represent a major change in the powers granted them by tradition and law in the 1930s and forties. What happened? How did courts get away with it in a country that has continued to give allegiance to representative democracy, that is, to rule by elected, rather than nonelected, officials?

To answer these questions we must tell, for the third time, a story we have already told first in terms of ethics and political philosophy and second in terms of law. This time we will tell it in terms of popular political movements and ideology. It is basically a story about American attitudes toward technical expertise. Of all the nations of the world, the United States is the one most preeminently identified with industrial technology. Its origins and rise to greatness correspond almost exactly in time to the industrial revolution, of which it has been the greatest beneficiary. The centrality of technology to American life has had an undeniable impact on our politics. It has always seemed self-evident to Americans that those who know how to do something ought to be in charge of doing it. Technology is related to technocracy, that is to the belief that those who know how to do things, technical experts, ought to rule. Technocratic and democratic ideas have always coexisted in American thinking about politics.

At the very founding of the Republic, there were two basic visions of the kind of public administration appropriate to the new nation. One vision was associated with the Federalists and particularly with Alexander Hamilton.[2] The new nation had public business to conduct and public property to manage. It followed that the administration of public affairs ought to be in the hands of persons expert in the management of affairs. The government's business ought to be conducted by that small set of persons who had proven themselves expert at business management. Those persons would necessarily be drawn from among the commercial and financial establishments of the great centers of business like Boston, New York, and Philadelphia and from among the great planters who managed large agricultural enterprises.

The opposing view was associated with the anti-Federalists, later Democrats, and particularly with Andrew Jackson.[3] The Federalists really spoke of public *business*; the Jacksonians of *public* business. In a democracy, the people should conduct their own affairs. Therefore public administration should be done by everyday people from the community, mostly small farmers and storekeepers and workers. To insure that they stayed everyday people, persons chosen to be government officials should hold government office for only a short time and then return to their everyday lives to be replaced by other plain citizens. For the Federalists, public administration was a complex matter requiring experts. Jacksonians thought that it was mostly simple common sense that anyone could do. Jackson's name is indelibly linked to "rotation in office" and the "spoils system." Just plain folks should rotate in and out of government office. When one political party won an election, its partisans should take over public administration. When the other party won, all the old public employees should be fired and replaced by the partisans of the newly elected party.

In general, the Jacksonian view prevailed until long after the

Civil War. It was in opposition to that view that the Progressive movement that began in the 1880s pushed its program of civil service reform. With the Progressives, the Hamiltonian view of government by experts took on a markedly technological character. Rotation and spoils, the Progressives argued, led, at the very least, to inefficient government. Most often they led to graft and corruption and political machines that served the highest bidder rather than the public interest. Such machines had no other interest than getting their people elected so that they could steal from the public treasury.

The Progressive solution was to separate public administration from politics.[4] Administration was to be turned over to a career civil service recruited by an objective system of written examinations controlled by an independent civil service commission. The examinations would test technical competence to do particular jobs. Public administration would become nonpartisan, efficient, and scientific. As the Progressives often said, "There is no Republican or Democratic way to pave a street, only the right way."

At the level of local government, the great lasting monument to Progressivism is the nonpartisan city manager and county administrator system now used in thousands of American locales. This system was designed to break the powers of corrupt big city machines. The basic functions of local government were not really political but technical—street maintenance, garbage collection, water supply, sewers, public health, and police and fire protection. Not a mayor heading a Democratic or Republic machine, but a nonpartisan expert managing a team of qualified engineers, doctors, and other technically trained people should run the city.

At state and national levels, civil service reform is our great Progressive heritage. The federal Pendleton Civil Service Act provides for the United States Civil Service Commission to oversee a body of civil servants who have life tenure in their jobs. They are selected by a system that requires government agencies to hire those most qualified to do particular government jobs on the basis of their education, past job experience, and scores on technical examinations. The typical executive-level civil servant in the United States is not a faithful worker for one of the two parties, or the child of an elite political family, or even someone with an advanced degree in public administration or management. Instead, typically, such people are graduates of state universities with bachelors or advanced degrees in poultry science, forestry, safety engineering, education, chemistry, or the like and many years of experience in the particular government agency which they now manage.

The Progressive creed was experts in the service of the public and government as essentially a set of technical services provided to the citizenry. Technocracy, not democracy, was what America needed, at least in the sphere of executive branch public administration. In the legislatures, where politics was supposed to reign, Progressives believed in democracy. And above the local level, Progressivism was identified with strong, popularly elected chief executives, that is, governors and presidents. Teddy Roosevelt and Woodrow Wilson were standard-bearers of the Progressive vision of strong, popularly elected presidents heading administrations of experts. In the twenties, the Republican party turned to the great engineer and manager, Herbert Hoover, to rehabilitate its reputation after the sometimes corrupt and always mediocre presidencies of two run-of-the-mill politicians, Harding and Coolidge.

As our succession to the presidency—Teddy Roosevelt, Taft, Wilson, Harding, Coolidge, Hoover—indicates, Progressives did not always win and technocracy did not become the unrivaled vision of public administration. From the time of the Hamilton-Jackson contrast until today, two rival visions attract Americans. One sees public administration as politics to be done like other politics by political party leaders whose fate is decided by the voters. The other sees public administration as the provision of technical services to be done by technical experts. It is not a matter of the two visions alternating, each replacing the other for a few years or decades. Both are always present in the American mind, but sometimes we emphasize one and at other times the other. At one of the times Americans seemed most disillusioned and bewildered by their government, they chose a president, Jimmy Carter, who presented himself as both a down-home peanut farmer and a nuclear engineer.

The New Deal was one of the great triumphs of the Progressive vision. In politics, Franklin Delano Roosevelt continued the Progressive, now Democratic, theory of the strong presidency. The part of the New Deal we tend to remember best is this identification of democracy with a small d, the Democratic party with a big D, and a strong presidency spelled FDR. The country was to be saved from the depression by the strong democratic and Democratic leadership of FDR. But the New Deal also taught that the country was to be saved from the depression by the multiplication of bold new government programs of spending, rehabilitation, and regulation, the creation of many new government agencies and the expansion of existing ones. A great flock of experts in agriculture, finance, social welfare, and other fields descended on Washington.

One of the key techniques of the New Deal was congressional passage of major new statutes that delegated sweeping discretion over vast areas of American life to administrative agencies. These agencies were told very little more than that they should use their technical expertise to decide what was in the public interest. By the 1940s, when enough Roosevelt appointees had come to the federal bench, the orthodoxy of administrative law became judicial self-restraint. Judges should defer to the expertise of administrative agencies. The agencies knew how to run the railroads and the airlines and the banks and the stock market and how to revive agriculture and industry and should be let alone to do their jobs. This notion that experts in the service of democracy should be given their head was central to administrative law. That is why conservative anti-New Dealers did not want administrative law at all. They wanted the good old law of private property rights enforced by the good old courts.

Rejection of Technocracy

The New Deal ideal of government by experts that flourished in the 1930s and 1940s began to tarnish badly in the fifties. At least four interrelated doubts about technocracy began to arise. The first is usually called the "capture" theory. To understand capture, we must first look at a peculiar American phenomenon, the independent regulatory commission. One of the great innovations of the Progressives, the independent regulatory commission began with the Interstate Commerce Commission in 1888. Each of the three words, *independent, regulatory,* and *commission,* is significant.

First, *regulatory.* Whatever else they were, Progressives were firmly a part of American capitalism. The great economic enterprises of the United States were to be privately owned and operated and essentially governed by the forces of the free market. Where, for one reason or another, enterprises threatened to escape the discipline of the market, they were not to be owned by the government, but to be subjected to government regulation. Basic decisions and day-to-day management were to remain in the hands of private entrepreneurs. Government agencies were to be armed with various carrots and sticks that could be employed to insure that the companies' pursuit of private gain remained compatible with the public interest. The railroad regulation that the ICC was set up to do meant that railroads were to remain privately owned but were not to gouge the farmers unfairly. The farmers needed regulatory protection because many of them were dependent on a single railroad to send their grain and livestock to market and so were not protected by competition between railroads. The ICC was to set fair freight rates, that is, rates that gave the railroads a profit, but not the excessive profit that they might have drawn from their quasi-monopolistic position.

So much for *regulatory;* on to *independent.* The Progressives wanted regulation in the public interest and thus regulation by experts. They did not want regulation by hack Jacksonian-style politicians who would use regulatory power to feather their own nest and that of their party. So they wanted the commissions to be free of partisan political control by either Congress or the president. Thus the commissions typically were set up to be headed by five or more commissioners appointed by the president with the advice and consent of the Senate for staggered seven-year (or longer) terms. Thus each commissioner served longer than the president who appointed him or her and each president had the opportunity to appoint only a minority of the commissioners within a single term of office. So much for the president. For its part, the politically partisan Congress was not supposed to write a detailed regulatory statute but was to provide a statute that declared the broad purpose that the railroads or other enterprise be regulated in the public interest. Such a statute should delegate to the expert commission the power to make all the regulations necessary to bring about that admirable state of affairs.

As for *commission,* that meant that the regulatory agencies were to be headed by a board of many persons rather than by one. One reason for the commission form has already been described. It made the commissions largely independent of any particular appointing president. More broadly, however, the commission form had been introduced at both local (police commissions, school boards) and national levels to insure against political partisanship and corruption. Normally, there would be both Republican and Democrat commissioners, insuring that neither party ran the commission for its own gain. It is, of course, harder (and more expensive) to bribe many persons than one, and the commissioners could watch each other for corruption.

The New Deal created a number of new independent regulatory commissions like the National Labor Relations Board and the Securities and Exchange Commission. It expanded the powers of several of the older commissions like the ICC, which was instructed to regulate railroads, truck lines, and barge lines to preserve the inherent advantages to the public of each.

With its theories of strong presidential leadership, the New Deal was not quite as enthusiastic about the independence of the commissions as the old Progressives had been. The New Dealers viewed the independent regulatory commission form as the price they had to pay to get huge new sectors of the economy under the regulatory umbrella of the federal government. Whenever they could, the New Dealers got Congress to delegate to regular bureaus of regular executive departments directly responsible to the president the same sort of sweeping discretion to make rules that it had given to commissions.

The capture theory really began with detailed studies of the oldest of the independent regulatory commissions, the ICC.[5] The ICC had been set up to regulate the railroads which appeared to have been doing bad things to the farmers. Looking back over the whole period from 1888 to the 1940s, however, observers began to see that the ICC had done awfully well by the railroads. Indeed, the railroads were enthusiastic supporters of the Commission. The trouble seemed to be that when a government agency regulates a particular industry, over time the agency tends to see the world more and more the way the industry sees it. It begins to regulate in the interest of the regulated.

There are a number of reasons why such capture of the regulator by the regulatee may occur. The regulated industry has a more direct, continuous, and intense interest than any other group in gaining access to and influencing the regulatory agency. So it will expend more time, money and energy in doing so. In other words, capture theory is an aspect of pluralist political theory. If public policy is made by group struggle, then regulatory agencies will be captured by regulated groups because those groups will struggle harder than anyone else.

A second explanation of capture rests more on social psychology than on political theory, but is compatible with the pluralist explanation. Those persons who do the regulating see and talk to those they regulate more often than anyone else. The regulatory people come to know more about and be more involved in day-to-day changes and problems in the industry they regulate than any other people in the whole country except those who work in the regulated industry. There was a time, many years ago, when American foreign service officers spent most of their lives in a single foreign country. The advantage of the arrangement was that each officer learned an enormous amount about that country. It was discovered, however, that after an American diplomat had spent twenty years in France trying to get the

French to do what the Americans wanted them to do, he had actually turned into a French diplomat trying to get the Americans to do what the French wanted them to do. Having lived in France so long, by imperceptible degrees the American had come to see the world the way the French did and to have lost touch with his homeland. So the Foreign Service began to rotate its officers, having them serve three years at home and then three years in a foreign country. Each overseas assignment might be to a different country. Having lived in the railroads for twenty years, it is easy to see how an ICC bureaucrat could come to believe that the railroads needed lots of carrots and no sticks.

A third explanation of capture is more economic in character. Regulation is regulation, not public ownership of industry in the socialist mode. Regulatory legislation is aimed at government intervention to move private management in certain directions and stop it from moving in others. Because regulation presupposes private ownership and thus private investment, regulatory legislation must include among its goals maintaining the industry in sufficient health to attract private investors who have the option of investing in other industries including nonregulated ones. Regulatory agencies will necessarily have a continuous concern for the well-being of the industry they regulate. The Interstate Commerce Act was designed to insure that the railroads made only a fair rate of return on their investment rather than exploiting the farmers. Put slightly differently, the Act told the ICC to set rates in such a way as to insure that the railroads made a profit. In 1888, no other industry enjoyed the protection of a special government agency to set prices to insure that it made a profit. In a sense, the traditional regulatory agencies were captured because the regulatory statutes themselves provided that the agency had a special responsibility for acting in behalf of the regulated industry.

So perhaps it was wrong to allow the technocrats in the agencies wide discretion. They might be captured and use their discretion to serve the regulated industry rather than the public.

Closely akin to capture theories are theories of "professional deformation."[6] If a government official was born on a small Ohio farm, has a degree in poultry science from Ohio State, got his first job as a field advisor with the United States Department of Agriculture working out of its Columbus office, and ended up as chief of the poultry division of the department, he is likely to think that chickens, and those who grow them, are far more important to the nation than the rest of us do. The aeronautical engineer who has spent her whole career in the Federal Aviation Agency is likely to feel the same way about planes. Each agency of government is likely to confuse its special interest with the general interest, to think that what is good for chicken farmers or the aerospace industry necessarily is also good for the country.

Theories of capture and professional deformation were two major reasons for distrusting technocratic government. A third had to do with the age of bureaucrats or the life cycle of regulatory agencies. Again it was the work on the first big regulatory agency, the ICC, that suggested life cycle theories. An agency is first established and its program defined by a congressional statute. If there weren't a lot of initial enthusiasm for the program, the statute wouldn't have passed in the first place. When the new agency created by the statute is set up, it naturally recruits young people who are enthusiastic about the agency's program. And there is a lot of public attention to what the agency is doing. Over the years, congressional and public interest wane and enthusiasms are worn down by day-to-day routine concerns. Capture begins to occur because over the years the agency sees the set of people directly affected by their program constantly and everyone else more and more occasionally. As the agency becomes more and more humdrum, the new generations of bureaucrats it attracts are less and less dedicated to the original programmatic vision. Old agencies tend to be captured, to acquire a distorted perspective and to lose their energy. Even if we believe in technocracy, in rule by people who know, it doesn't seem very attractive to leave government to this particular set of knowers.

A fourth and final reason that people began to lose faith in the New Deal formula of rule by experts involves doubts not about government bureaucracies but about technology itself and therefore about technocrats. Obviously, science and technology are key values and endeavors of Western civilization. The United States is the most committed to these values of all the Western nations. Yet there has always been a certain ambivalence toward technology and the urbanized, industrialized and perhaps dehumanized society that it brings in its wake. There are recurrent waves of fear that machines will replace human workers and drive them into poverty. An early nineteenth-century English workers' movement sought to smash the new machines and we worry now about automation.

At another level we experience yearnings for a return to a simpler society closer to nature. The nineteenth-century romanticism of Keats and Shelley, the twentieth-century romanticism of D. H. Lawrence, the "alternative life style" and "commune" movement of the sixties, and the search for "community" among modern political philosophers are all varities of this ambivalence. The central thinker of the critical legal studies movement, which gains such disproportionate attention in legal circles today and is largely Marxist, turns out not to be a Marxist but a utopian calling for a society of small communities magically released from the alienating forces of modern technological life.[7] Perhaps the clearest manifestation of the ambivalence is our life style. Both in Europe and the United States, everyone who can afford to do so either has an apartment in the city and a weekend place in the country or lives in the somewhat artificial "nature" of the suburbs while commuting by the technological magic of trains and freeways to the technological jobs of the cities.

Sometimes this ambivalence is reflected in waves of enthusiasm for or distrust of technology. A great wave of technological enthusiasm broke over us around World War II. Immediately preceding the war, during the depression, the dreams of most Americans were focussed on getting our industrial economy going again. Far more people than wanted to were sitting watching the grass, and the bills, grow. Our vast technological capacity appeared to be what allowed the "democracies" to beat the Fascists in World War II, incidentally putting everyone back to work, and culminating in the final triumph of science over the war lords, the atom bomb. In the aftermath of the war, America's greatest foreign policy achievement was the Marshall Plan, the rebuilding of European technology to block Soviet expansion in the West.

In the 1960s, however, we went through an antitechnology wave that at the time was sometimes referred to as "the greening of America." Preserving the environment, reviving endangered species, ending air and water pollution, living more simple, natural lives by moving to an Oregon commune or wearing blue jeans or eating granola became central to American life. They were particularly important to a generation of youth that could not even imagine unemployment and poverty except among the oppressed whom they were going to liberate. They also became serious policy goals for intellectuals and politicians newly sensitive to the down side of the rapid, technology-based, economic development of the 1950s.

This great concern with what technology was doing to us rather than for us was in part a late awakening to the tremendous ecological damage caused by the extremely rapid economic development of World War II and the postwar period. In part it was a response to the very prosperity created by development. In the sixties, the United States appeared to be producing so much of everything and to be so incredibly prosperous that it could afford all the various drains on industrial productivity necessary to fix the environment, uplift the poor, and allow all those who were so inclined to live an alternative life style—that is to live very well while producing very little. There appeared to be no need to think about the trade-offs between the greening of America and further economic and technological development because America seemed to be more than sufficiently economically and technologically developed.

Even the slightest touch of green thinking was likely to bring with it much more than a touch of suspicion of technicians and technocratic government. Because technicians had devoted much of their lives to learning and practicing their technology, they were necessarily prone to exaggerate its importance and resist its restriction. The Corps of Engineers, for instance, went from a hero agency that prevented floods and drained swamps to a villain agency that assaulted natural beauty and destroyed wetlands. Its engineer's fascination for replacing the beautiful disorder of nature with the beautiful order of reinforced concrete had somehow to be curbed.

It was here that the green current and the anti-federalist or Jacksonian current mingled to create the greatest distrust of technocracy. The first great symptom was the denunciation of the "military-industrial complex" that began even in the 1950s, signalled by President Eisenhower's retirement address. That "complex" was an alliance between the military and industry to produce the most massive military technology ever created. It had produced the United States victories in World War II. Nevertheless, the greatest commander of that war was warning that the technological experts in government, that is, the soldiers and civilians of the Defense Department, were forming an unholy alliance with the defense contracting industries. That alliance was diverting an unwarranted share of the nation's wealth into profits for the industry and elaborate and expensive toys for the military. The Department of Defense had been captured by the aerospace industry. The technical experts at big war were merrily running an arms race.

Now, at least in one context, the expert no longer appeared to be what the Progressive believers in rule by experts had portrayed, a neutral, objective technician who harnessed his or her expertise to the pursuit of the public interest. Instead, the experts, precisely because they were expert, had a special interest in the particular technology in which they had acquired expertise.

It was soon discovered that this phenomenon existed far beyond defense policy. Government highway engineers loved to build highways even where people didn't want them and irrigation specialists constantly sought out new deserts to water. All government experts seemed to have a natural tendency to form alliances with those in the private sector who shared the same interests—the ICC expert in locomotives with the rail-roads who owned and operated them; the army tank expert with the auto manufacturer who built them. Far from insuring that an agency could withstand capture and pursue the public interest, staffing it with experts insured the reverse. The Progressives and their New Deal successors had taught that agencies should be granted very broad discretion because of their expertise. It now began to appear that agencies should be particularly watched and controlled because of their expertise.

If the nation were suffering from too much and indiscriminate technological development and could afford to curb it, and if government experts themselves were deeply implicated in self-interested pursuit of more development, then who was to do the curbing? Above all, who was to guard the guardians? Who was to control the government experts who were supposed to regulate their counterparts in the private sector, but shared too many special interests with them to do so?

Enter the judge. Judges are not expert at anything except law, and law is just words. By virtue of education and experience judges knew nothing about any of the technologies that had created the modern world. They knew no nuclear engineering or chemistry or even poultry science. And judges not only had the wonderful virtue of not knowing anything, they were also wielders of government power who could wield that power to overcome technocracy, now seen as the tyranny of experts. Most importantly, judges traditionally performed the legitimate government role of judicial review of the agencies, a role that had been limited, but also consolidated, by the Administrative Procedures Act.

At the height of the New Deal, judicial interference with administrative agencies had appeared as a kind of hubris. Those wedded to old magic rituals got in the way of those who knew how to do what needed to be done to get the nation out of the depression and to win the war. By the sixties, that same interference appeared as the intervention of the nonexpert protector of the public against those corrupted into the selfish pursuit of special interest by their special expertise. The judge had been converted from industrial idiot to postindustrial hero. As postindustrial hero, the judge felt fully justified and popularly authorized to conduct the enormous transformation of administrative law of the 1960s and 1970s. This transformation made the judge a senior partner to the agencies in taking a hard look at the policies espoused by the agencies' experts.

The linkage between the greening of the sixties and seventies and the new judicial activism of that period need not be only a highly general historical inference drawn from the then prevalent currents of opinion. Robert Rabin[8] has pointed out that the new judicial activism arose quite directly and specifically out of the litigation spawned by the National Environmental Protection Act's environmental impact statement requirement and the Clean Air Act's many detailed air quality requirements. He argues that two features of these and other environmental statutes were crucial. First, they demanded that the agencies take into account intangible values such as scenic beauty. Second, they demanded that the agencies reach definitive policies in the face of, and in spite of, high levels of uncertainty about risk. These two features tended to dramatize the already existing suspicion of the agencies as both captured and "professionally deformed." Why should judges defer to agency expertise when the issue was intangible values that the experts did not particularly value and information was so uncertain that it could not yield the technologically correct answers that were the reason for deferring to experts in the first place? As Shep Melnick[9] has shown, the judges of the D.C. and other circuits shared the dedication to environmental values of the day. The environmental cases brought the judges' strong proenvironmental policy urges toward judicial activism together with issues of intangible values and uncertain risk that triggered their strongest antiexpert urges toward judicial activism. The environmental cases thus became the vehicle for enthusiastic judicial acceptance of the role of postindustrial hero.

Having reached hero status among those greening America, the judges then reaped equal kudos from the opponents of the green. Regulated industries quickly learned to use the hard look doctrine too. That doctrine demanded that agencies engage in adjudicatory processes and synoptic decision making, which took a lot of time, slowed the pace of new regulation, and provided those regulated with endless quibbles on which to base court challenges to the new rules that delayed their enforcement even longer. Even more important than procedural review under the hard look doctrine was synoptic substantive review. If courts demanded that agencies take everything into account, they were demanding that agencies take into account the costs as well as the benefits of the new regulatory statutes. Regulated industries could use synoptic judicial review to bring forward as defenses all the economic factors that green forces wished to ignore.[10] So in the end, both environmentalists and the polluting industries came to insist on hard-look judicial review that demanded that agencies reach synoptically correct rules.

The Triumph of the Judiciary

We are now ready to put our four stories together and summarize how the court supervision of agencies that we call administrative law got to be what it was in the sixties and seventies. In response to the depression and World War II, the New Deal greatly expanded the federal bureaucracy and brought to a dramatic culmination the Progressive ideal of technocratic government. Under the general control of a popularly elected president, vast amounts of policy-making discretion were to be delegated to expert administrative agencies. Conservative opponents of the New Deal sought to fight against this model by reasserting the Diceyan model of the individual's right to be protected against agencies by the courts. The result was a compromise embodied in the APA. When impinging upon the particular interests of particular individuals, agencies were to act as much like courts as possible. When making more general policies, they were to exercise law-making discretion under only the loosest court supervision designed to control the most extreme abuses of their delegated powers.

In the 1950s, however, pluralist ideals began to challenge the New Deal vision. Politics was no longer seen as individuals voting for a democratic and Democratic president supervising experts who made technically correct decisions in the public interest. Instead, politics was seen as groups struggling with one another to achieve government actions that would serve their group interests. Such a theory was derived from and compatible with utilitarian ethics. If right and wrong, good and bad, were merely matters of preference, then a political process that "satisficed" group preferences was a good process yielding good policies. The role of the agencies was still one of expert neutrality, but neutrality took on a new meaning. The agencies were not to exercise their own discretion to choose for themselves policies that served the common good. Instead, they were to serve as neutral arena managers and referees. They were to provide a place in which the group struggle could occur and turn the outcomes of that struggle into public policy.

Because the very expertise of the agency was likely to yield excessive agency favoritism for certain groups, the nature of judicial review changed too. It was no longer reserved for the rare occasions when an expert ran amok and had to be declared an arbitrary and capricious lunatic. Now the nonexpert, truly neutral judge was to review far more actively and create a body of administrative law that insured equal access to all the groups. Judges would insure that agencies really listened to everyone by requiring the agencies to respond to everything every group said.

The pluralist critique of technocratic government then itself fell under a shadow. First, it was noticed that no matter how hard everyone tried, some groups seemed to be more equal than others. The courts responded by pushing their demands for equality of group access to the extreme. The agencies must make a perfect record of finding every group and responding to every last blink and nod that every group displayed.

A more fundamental attack on pluralism, however, came from a postconsequentialist ethics that insisted that the good was not merely a matter of pure, irreconcilable and noncomparable personal and group preferences. Some statements of the good and some public policies were better than others. They were not better merely because they were preferred by more individuals or groups. There were public values; some policies were more in the public interest than others; there was a common good above and beyond the transient product of the previous inning of the continuous group struggle. Government technocrats had betrayed the common good. They were pushing their own and their private sector allies' interests in technological development to a point where they threatened such basic values as the survival of the natural world, the purity and beauty of the environment, and the basic humanity of human beings.

Thus there must be a final step for the judge, a step beyond merely insisting that the agency experts correct their professional deformations, avoid capture, and listen to all the groups. The final step was to insist that the agencies make right decisions clearly and consciously directed by properly articulated public values and resting on correct technical analysis. The ultimate job of the judge was to insure that agencies made their decisions synoptically whenever they could reasonably be expected to do so. It followed that one of the basic duties of agencies was to submit to the courts a record of decision that would allow the courts to check on agency synopticism.

To return to where we started, it was the duty of the agency to deliberate in the way a moral philosopher armed with technical as well as moral knowledge would deliberate, and by deliberation to choose the good. It was the duty of courts to insure that the agencies had deliberated rightly. The only way that courts seemed able to perform that duty was to themselves deliberate. By the 1980s, it had become the fashion among the youngest, brightest scholars of administrative law and the most active judges to call for deliberative agencies overseen by deliberative courts.[11] As we shall see later, however, those who believe in agency and court deliberation do not all believe that deliberation and synopticism are necessarily synonymous.

The Engines of Change

It is fashionable to present law as mere ideology, as a kind of professional mumbo jumbo seeking to legitimate and elevate the immediate interests of those political players in a position to tap legal skills. What we have seen is that administrative law is not merely legal ideology in this sense. Instead, administrative law has been responsive to major movements in moral philosophy, in political theory, and in general public attitudes about technological development. Administrative law has also been subject to certain relatively autonomous dynamics of internal legal development.

Following the Diceyan prescription there had initially been no administrative law. Then, by incorporating existing agency practice into law, the APA created an administrative law. That law was fairly detailed for agency adjudication, rudimentary for rule making, and lumped everything else government did into one category—discretion—for which it provided almost no law at all. Quite apart from any changes in other kinds of thought, surely we would have expected a community of lawyers and judges as large and influential as that of the United States to come up with some legal response to the explosion of executive agencies and government regulation that was a core feature of the New Deal, and it did in the APA.

Once the APA was in place, it was almost inevitable that courts would labor to create a detailed set of legal requirements to fill out its rudimentary provisions on agency rule making. For the APA provided just enough judicial review of rule making to insure that the courts would get a substantial number of rule making review cases, but not enough to tell the courts how to decide them. In this situation it was natural for the courts to devise a lot of law of their own prescribing how they should review agency rule making and thus how agencies should make rules. For any directive a reviewing court gives to itself as to what it should look for in agency rule making necessarily is also a directive to the agency as to how it should make rules.

So quite apart from pluralism and postpluralism and postconsequentialism and the greening of America, some growth in the judge-made administrative law of rule making was to be expected in the sixties and seventies. The rapidity of that growth, its initial pluralist content, its seizure for judges of the senior partnership over the agencies, and its shift from incrementalism to synopticism are, of course, largely the products of these outside movements that we have discussed at such length. Some kind of change was inevitable given the internal dynamics of an independent judiciary, an active bar and a regulatory system that provides enormous incentives to private parties to finance litigation designed to engender such change. The directions and substance of the changes, however, were largely determined by forces beyond the lawyers' control.

Chapter Four

Regulation and Deregulation

In this chapter we are going to examine administrative law as ideology, as a way of clothing particular political interests and agendas with legal legitimacy. In doing so, however, we always should remember that the persons espousing various administrative law doctrines and various roles for the reviewing courts are rarely mere cynical ideologues looking for big words to camouflage their political maneuvers. More typically, lawyers, judges, and commentators are caught up in broader changes in moral and political philosophy, social thought, and legal theory. What they are up to is ideological combat, but it is also thinking and writing about the broader issues we have spent so much time on. It is also a part of the natural tendency of administrative law to catch up with what is actually going on in government.

Of course, there has always been a significant ideological dimension to administrative law. The conflict between the Diceyans and the New Dealers was a conflict between conservatives and liberals and between Republicans and Democrats. The opponents of the New Deal used rule-of-law and individual-rights rhetoric and denounced the "statism" of continental administrative law as a way of attacking the expansion of the executive branch and presidential power. Those expansions were the great successes of the Democratic Party of President Franklin Delano Roosevelt. The New Deal spoke the Progressive language of neutral technocracy, of the discretion due to expertise. At the same time it was basically concerned with transferring law-making power from a Congress that was never entirely under New Deal control after 1936 to an executive branch whose newly created and/or expanded staffs were entirely loyal to FDR.

The basic story of ideological conflict that we need to follow is a somewhat later one and revolves about "deregulation." Before we look at deregulation, however, we must return to regulation.

We saw earlier that regulation is essentially a device of a capitalist economy. Private ownership, entrepreneurship, and management are combined with limited government intervention. This intervention is designed to make up for lapses and imperfections in the control over private endeavor provided by the discipline of a free market economy. The New Deal had expanded government regulation. In the sixties and seventies, large numbers of Americans came to believe that health, safety, and environmental concerns ought to be moved to the top of the public policy agenda. They, too, chose the route of expansion of the government's regulatory apparatus.

We have seen that by the sixties, serious doubts had begun to arise about the traditional pattern of alloting broad regulatory discretion to expert agencies, each of which was also responsible for the health of the particular industry it regulated. Capture, professional deformation, and ties between agency and industry experts all seemed to threaten the Progressive model of regulation. Yet those who wanted to "green" America did not want to shift its economy from private to public ownership. They remained in the American capitalist tradition. Indeed, it was widely noted that socialist states in which industry was government owned hardly had outstanding health, safety, and environmental records. So long as ownership remained private, regulation appeared to be the only available mode of achieving green goals even when distrust of regulators abounded.

The New Regulatory Statutes

The tensions between enthusiasm for health, safety and environmental regulation on the one hand and distrust of the regulators on the other account for the nature of the major

regulatory statutes of the sixties and seventies.[1] A new generation of younger congressmen and women, enthusiastic about
the postindustrial values sweeping America, began to write
such new statutes as the National Highway Safety Act, the
Environmental Protection Act, the Clean Air and Clean Water
statutes and the Occupational Safety and Health Act. They also
passed strengthening amendments to the food and drug and
Federal Trade Commission statutes. Most of these statutes have
certain basic features in common.

First of all, in their preambles and general provisions, they
announce ambitious aspirations: that American workers have a
safe workplace, that new pollution be prevented and existing
pollution be rolled back until the air and water are clean, and
that the risks created by industrial products and processes be
reduced to zero. To label these goals as aspirations, however, is
to become a part of the ideological battle. For to label them aspirations is to suggest that these were ideal or utopian or far off
goals toward which Congress was only asking for progress. The
statutes did not use aspirational language. They appeared to
give definite commands to the agencies they created, like the
Occupational Safety and Health Administration and the
Environmental Protection Agency, to achieve safety and a clean
environment, if not immediately, then pretty damn quick.[2]

If the great declaratory sections of these statutes are to be
viewed as aspirational, it is not because they use the language of
long-term goals. Rather, it is because they demand so much that
it is not reasonable to believe that all the things demanded could
be quickly accomplished, no matter what the statutes say. On
the other hand, Congress did not appear to be in the mood to be
"reasonable." It seemed to expect that public values be achieved
now. The statutes reflected the new preoccupation with objective values. For all the talk of "satisficing" and incrementalism
and the need to placate all the groups, if all the fish in the river
died, that was wrong, and what was right was cleaning up the
river.

Alongside these commitments to doing right right now, there
is a second level of considerably more detailed provisions. They

are often referred to as "agency forcing" and "technology forcing." Congress wanted its goals reached, but it did not think it could simply make pollution and danger crimes and hand everything over to federal prosecutors. Attaining safety and environmental purity would require the development of detailed rules and standards. These rules and standards would have to be applied to thousands of particular situations. Hundreds of thousands of business firms and other organizations would have to be pulled and prodded to achieve compliance. So the new statutes typically created new agencies to carry them out.

Congressional suspicion of expert agencies led to some big changes from the Progressive and New Deal model. No longer were new agencies given maximum discretion under a vague general statutory command to pursue the public interest. The new statutes said a lot more and were a lot more specific.[3] They contained relatively detailed standards for how clean was clean enough. Often they contained timetables specifying when the agency was to come up with and enforce even more specific standards. They sometimes even prescribed the scientific methods through which the standards were to be derived. And if the agency still did not seem to get the message, Congress would sometimes spell it out, as it did in Clean Air Act amendments that required the agency to require the "lowest possible emission rate" and the "best available control technology."[4] All of this was obviously designed to hold captured, lazy, and/or self-interested experts up to the mark of vigorously pursuing statutory goals.

Congress may even have been more suspicious of the agencies than it needed to be. Agencies like OSHA and EPA were newly created by their statutes and naturally tended to recruit safety and environmental enthusiasts to fill their many new positions. If agencies are energetic when young and lazy when old, a lot of regulatory energy would be expected from the new agencies. Also OSHA and EPA, unlike the old single-industry regulators, regulated all industries and so were less easily captured by any one. They did not have the intimate and continuous relationship with a single industry that leads the regulator to take on the point of view of the people being regulated. They were not supposed to take care of the economic health of any particular industry. Indeed they were dedicated to a single value, such as safety or the environment, rather than having to balance many values as the older agencies did. So if they were going to be "deformed" in any direction, it was likely to be toward overenthusiasm for that value.[5]

Nevertheless, Congress not only engaged in a great deal of relatively detailed control over the agencies, it somewhat hesitantly and uncertainly used two other strategies to improve the new agencies' regulatory performance. Of the various new agencies, it made only a few independent commissions. OSHA and EPA were single-headed agencies. Their heads were appointed by the president, and not for a long fixed term. OSHA is a part of the Labor Department. EPA reports directly to the president. It was hoped that single agency heads under direct presidential control would be more vigorous enforcers than independent commissioners had been. At the same time, however, these statutes made these agencies somewhat more independent of the president than executive agencies normally are, so that there would be less danger of presidential pressure slowing them down.

The final congressional step to invigorate the new regulators was the most vague and uncertain, the least complete and has caused the most subsequent dispute over just how far Congress intended to go. We have seen that one of the largest chinks in the armor of earlier single-industry regulators had been that they became responsible not only for regulating their industry but for keeping it economically healthy. EPA and OSHA were not single-industry regulators and thus, by their very nature, were not concerned with keeping "their" industry profitable. In some statutory provisions, either explicitly or more often by implication, Congress suggested that it wanted safety and environmental cleanliness achieved no matter what, even if some businesses or indeed some whole industries had to shut down. Some factories or industries might find it physically impossible to meet the tough standards contemplated by the statutes. Others might not be able to meet them and still make a profit. Others yet might be able to meet them only by investing so much in rebuilding and re-equipping old facilities that it was cheaper to shut them down and build new ones. But the new facilities might not necessarily be constructed in the same town or state as the old ones had been.

Moreover, in order to maintain existing levels of air and water purity, some whole states and regions, particularly in the West, might have to forego any further industrial development. And, if you took everything in the statutes seriously, some cities like Los Angeles would simply have to shut down because they generated so much air pollution. The statutes clearly did not require EPA and OSHA to keep every factory or industry or city or state economically healthy. The statutory language went some way toward requiring them and other agencies to meet their "green" goals no matter what the economic impact. It was difficult to say, however, just how far the statutes went in that direction.

The new statutes evidenced great distrust, not only of the vigor of government regulators, but of technologists as such. They were "technology forcing" as well as agency forcing. Regulation, unlike government ownership, leaves not only industrial production but the bulk of new technological development in private hands. Those who want a cleaner, safer world often encounter catch-22. Given existing technologies there may be no way to make certain processes and machines cleaner and safer. Yet the only companies with the investment capital and the know-how to invent new, cleaner, safer technologies are those that are now dirty and unsafe. If they invent the new technologies, they will no longer have the excuse they presently have for not meeting regulatory standards. So why should they try to develop the new technologies? And if they don't, nobody else can.

There have always been rumors of the automobile industry buying up and hiding patents for alternatives to the conventional internal-combustion gasoline engine. Similar rumors circulate about the same companies buying up and suppressing really effective smog-control devices for such engines so that they won't have to change their evil ways. Disappointing experience with the Wankel rotary engine and the failure of independent entrepreneurs to achieve a breakthrough in either reduced fuel consumption or smog control devices have not ended such rumors.

The dangers of such potential catch-22s were aggravated by the professional ties between experts in and out of government. The automotive engineer working for the government to produce safety and pollution regulations for vehicles had to come from somewhere. If she had the experience necessary to write such regulations, she probably would have gained it by working in the industry. Indeed, her engineering education and the very textbooks and manuals she consulted were pervaded by the Detroit point of view. It appeared unlikely that government technicians would force their private counterparts into technological breakthroughs. It was far more likely that all the technicians, government and private, would get together to tell the idiot laymen that they wouldn't be asking for such crazy things if they knew anything about technology.

To avoid catch-22, in a number of instances Congress mandated safety and pollution standards, such as those for auto emissions, that simply could not be met by existing technologies. Congress believed that, given sufficient incentives, the private sector would come up with new technologies. Having to shut down the auto industry appeared to be a sufficient negative incentive to get General Motors and the others moving down the technology trail. Technicians both inside and outside of government would be forced to stop hiding behind their expertise and get the job done.

Justice Frankfurter once said that the job of government agencies was to smooth the sharp corners off of congressional statutes as they administered them. These new statutes were full of agency and technology forcing provisions designed to keep the sharp corners on.

In addition to the great aspirational commands and detailed directions to agencies of these statutes, there was a third element. The safety, health, and environmental movements of the sixties and seventies were very strongly represented in Congress, but they were not absolutely overwhelming. In the congressional legislative process, even relatively small interests can hold out long enough against a majority to extract some kind of compromise and get some of what they want.

One of the reasons that these statutes could demand almost immediate achievement of big goals was that they assigned most of the cost to the private sector. When Congress mandates a big program that government pays for itself, like the B1 bomber, Congress knows that it will eventually have to come up with the tax money to pay for it. That tends to curb some of its enthusiasm for big programs. Health, safety, and environmental regulation costs the government relatively little—the salaries of the regulators. The billions of dollars in costs of substituting expensive safe chemicals for cheap dangerous ones and installing huge fans to suck fumes out of the factory and scrubbers to clean the smoke as it comes out of the stacks do not fall on Congress. Instead they fall on private industry and on particular areas of the country where jobs may be lost. So Congress can be very enthusiastic because someone else pays the bills. But the someone else is not going to be very enthusiastic, and the someone else has some representation in Congress.

Even some of those who favored the new statutes, like labor unions which were particularly enthusiastic about protecting the health and safety of their members, were anxious to avoid Fearless Fosdick regulation. Fosdick was a maniacal comic strip cop who thwarted would-be murderers by himself shooting their potential victims. If the local factory on which the whole economy of a town depended shut down because it could not meet EPA standards and still turn a profit, there might be no one left in the town to enjoy all that clean air and pure water. There were some members of Congress who feared the creation of clean, safe ghost towns in their districts.

There were many members of Congress with some concern for the costs and job losses that rigorous enforcement of environmental, health, and safety standards might require, particularly when no current technology existed to meet those standards. So many of the new statutes ultimately contained a number of fudge clauses.[6] In some instances, Congress indicated that it was permissible for the enforcing agencies to make regulations that put the least profitable and/or most dangerous or polluting factories in an industry out of business, but not regulations that might shut down the whole industry. In others, Congress indicated that if something really turned out to be technologically impossible, regulations might be softened or delayed. In one famous instance, auto exhaust emissions, where Congress refused to build any fudge factor into its statute, Congress itself ended up having to amend the statute every few years to allow for further delays. In other instances, Congress inserted language to suggest that agency regulations should not end up imposing costs on industry that were entirely disproportionate to the amount of health, safety, or environmental protection gained.

It is extremely difficult to write such statutory language. Some of the proponents of the new statutes simply did not care how much they cost or how many people they put out of work. They were tired of having basic values like clean air compromised away. A few were using the statutes simply to express their hatred of corporate, capitalist, industrial, technocratic society. The more damage to it the better. Most did not want to spend a million dollars to buy a nickle's worth of new safety or shut down Pittsburgh in order to increase the number of fish in the Allegheny River.

When you do not trust agencies, experts, or technologists, however, it is extremely hard to state in a law that you want a little give, a little slack, a little reasonableness in enforcement without at the same time giving the people you distrust a lot of discretion. For instance the Clean Air Act Amendments of 1970 told the agency to set "a standard . . . which reflects the . . . emission limitation achievable through the application of the *best system* of emission reduction which (*taking into account the cost of achieving such reductions*) the Administration determines has been adequately demonstrated." Later amendments called upon it to require "*reasonably available* control technology."[7]

There was another aspect to this third level of statutory provisions. By the time the new statutes were being enacted, courts were beginning to impose rule-making record requirements. They were also beginning to use the arbitrary and capricious standard not only as a lunacy test but as a judicial demand that the agencies back their rules with strong factual support. Some of the new statutes themselves contained rule-making record requirements designed to assure access of environmental, safety, and consumer groups to the new agencies. Because the new statutes were agency-forcing and technology-forcing, they often contemplated agencies making rules on the basis of far from perfect knowledge. If the EPA waited to issue an air quality standard until we could write a perfect computer program of just how smog was generated and dissipated over the Los Angeles basin, we might have to wait forever for the standard.

Enthusiasts of the new programs wanted to soften the evidence requirements on the rule-making agencies even though they distrusted the agencies. Those fearful of the costs of the new programs wanted to make sure the agencies knew exactly what they were doing and what it would cost before they did it. As a result, a number of the new statutes contain special formulae for the degree of evidence necessary to support agency rules. One such formula is "best available evidence on the rule-making record as a whole." Such a formula might mean that, where an agency simply couldn't get the evidence it needed, it might proceed on the basis of its best guess. Or it might mean that even if the agency had enough evidence to show that it was not acting arbitrarily or capriciously in making a new rule, it needed even more evidence to make a rule under this particular statute.

Implementing the New Statutes

What we are seeing, then, is that the new regulatory statutes of the sixties and seventies were much longer and more detailed than most of their predecessors and contained a great many ambiguities and even contradictions. What appeared to be commanded in sweeping terms in the first level of these statutes often seemed to be qualified and even subjected to exemptions in the third level provisions. These third-level fudge factors themselves often were ambiguous and ill-defined. The specific standards of the second level often did not seem exactly to match the general commands. Now we can see why statutory interpretation recently has come to center stage in academic writing on administrative law. There is far more to interpret, it is far more difficult to interpret, and what needs interpreting is far more important to the regulators and the regulatees.[8]

Further problems arose when the agencies attempted to implement these statutes.[9] They required the agencies to write literally thousands of safety and pollution standards. Just how many parts of lead per million parts of air were workers allowed to breathe in a battery manufacturing plant? And was the required reduction to be achieved by installing an air cleaning system in the plant or requiring workers to wear respirators? How many cross braces of what thickness at what angles were to be required in a scaffolding that was four stories high and had to bear a weight of sixteen hundred pounds? How many gallons of treated sewage could a stream accept with a flow of twenty thousand gallons per minute before becoming too polluted to sustain fish life? And what level of fish life—the number of fish that were in the river last year after it had been polluted for twenty years or the number that might have been there before any towns had been built along the banks? In spite of the many agency and technology forcing provisions, agencies proved extremely slow in issuing standards. They sometimes took five or six years to issue ten or twelve standards when they should have issued hundreds.

A large part of the delay was to be attributed to the interaction of two factors. First, in spite of legislative commands that they do the impossible, it proved very difficult for the agencies to arrive at the facts they needed to set standards. It turned out to take more time, effort and money than the agency had available to discover just how much sediment there has to be in a particular stream before a particular kind of fish in that stream stops breeding.

The second factor was the way administrative law had been developing. The new safety, health, and environmental standards had to be made by the informal rule-making process. In the same years that the new statutes were being written, the courts and Congress, first in the name of perfecting pluralism, and then in the name of synopticism, were making more and more demands on the rule-making agencies. A standard setting procedure that required the agency first to respond to every comment of everybody who had the slightest interest and then to go on to gather every fact and consider every alternative could take a very long time indeed.[10]

So one problem of implementing the new statutes was simply writing the many supplementary rules and standards they required. A second was the high level of resistance by the regulated to agency enforcement. We have seen that part of Congress's enthusiasm for big-scale health, safety, and environmental regulation had stemmed from the fact that most of the costs would be borne by private industry rather than the taxpayers. Those very high costs, however, drove some industries to fight many of the regulations tooth and nail. And the complexity of the statutes, particularly their fudge factors, gave the regulated a lot of opportunities for at least arguably legal resistance. They would first fight it out with the agency and then go to court and fight it out all over again.

Faced with high levels of resistance, the agencies soon ran into the dark side of congressional enthusiasm for tough regulation at low cost to government. Those to whom the costs were assigned were prepared to put lots of money into fighting agency enforcement. Congress was not nearly as willing to pour government money into building up the research, standard-writing, and enforcement resources of the agencies. Seeking to get the most bang for their enforcement buck, some agencies began to seek compromises with the regulated industries. They allowed some deviation from the strictest standards in return for voluntary partial compliance by the industries and their good faith efforts to make progress toward the high statutory goals. Of course, when the agencies engaged in this kind of compromise, health and environmental groups immediately accused them of having been captured by the regulated. All this led to even more litigation.

The complexity of the statutes, the complexity of the technological knowledge needed to make them work, the high cost to industry and its consequent high propensity to resist, and the passion with which the health and environmental goals of the statutes were held by many Americans led to long and complex rule-making proceedings. These proceedings were followed by hard-fought and often compromised applications of the new rules and standards to particular industries and facilities.

The court-dictated movement of administrative law toward more and more demands on the rule-making and implementing agencies was one of the causes of regulatory complexity, delay, and incompleteness. But here we encounter a chicken-and-egg problem. For the litigation that arose from the new regulation was one of the factors pushing the courts toward making superpluralist and finally synoptic demands on the agencies. The large number of very, very interested parties, the complexity of the statutes, and the technological difficulty of setting air and water pollution and safety standards created an inevitable pressure on the courts to demand that the agencies listen to everybody, know everything and make the right rule.[11]

In the course of agency formulation and implementation of the new regulation, and of judicial review of agency action, certain splits and tensions became evident in both agencies and courts. EPA and OSHA were not brand new agencies in their entirety. They consisted in part of existing units of other departments, such as the Department of Agriculture, that were transferred to them. Some of these units showed signs of capture, professional deformation, and old age. Apart from these problems, even newly hired technicians imbued with enthusiasm for their newly created agency's mission may quickly come to resent and, in a sense, resist the agency's statute. If that statute is agency-forcing and technology-forcing, agency technicians often may find themselves in the position of saying that they do not yet have sufficient evidence of sufficient scientific validity to make the rules that the statute demands be made.

In many instances, the top echelons of the new agencies hired a lot of young lawyers very much wedded to the right values and totally unencumbered by technical knowledge or scruples, formed them into litigation sections and allowed the litigation sections to assume policy-making power. Lawyers ultimately partake of the same canons of truth as the rest of us, simply because they, too, are children of Western civilization. Nevertheless, the adversary method of finding truth that they are taught in law school is very different than the scientific method. Agency lawyers were very anxious to discover that version of truth that best justified vigorous agency pursuit of health, safety, and environmental goals. Agency scientists and technicians were far more anxious to discover that version of truth that would best pass the tests for truth that they had learned in the laboratory. Enthusiastic regulatory agency heads sometimes used their lawyers to end run their scientists. As a result, the rule-making and reviewing process became more legal and less scientific than it otherwise might have been.[12]

In the courts a different split became evident; it has been well documented in the work of Shep Melnick on air pollution.[13] Most of the appeals from the agency rule-making proceedings went to the D.C. Circuit. It tended to emphasize the sweeping commands and agency- and technology-forcing aspects of the statutes and to minimize considerations of cost and economic dislocation. Most of the lawsuits concerning the specific applications of these rules and standards to particular facilities and particular places were filed in federal district courts scattered all over the United States. They tended to pay far more attention to the fudge factors built into the original statutes. They were much less enthusiastic about requiring industry to do things that no one yet knew how to do. They were much more cost-conscious and more likely to permit substantial delays where the alternative seemed to be shutting down factories or limiting economic growth.

Particularly in the older industrial areas of the Northeast, factory owners often argued that it was impossible for their old plants to meet the new standards, or that they could not meet them and still make a profit. Often major corporations argued that it was more economically rational to shut down old plants that would cost a lot to bring up to new standards and build new ones. It was also more economically rational, however, to build the new ones in others parts of the country or abroad. The Northeast was faced with limited supplies of already heavily polluted water and air. Cities and towns often argued that they could meet new clean air and water standards only by radically cutting back on economic activity and thus throwing thousands of people out of work. In the mountain and desert states, entrepreneurs and local governments often argued that rules that required them to stay as clean as they were would make it impossible for them to have any economic growth. They did not necessarily want to remain pure and clean playgrounds for those grown rich on the industrial development of the older, dirtier states.

There were a great many accusations of Fearless Fosdick–style regulation. District courts tended to be fairly sympathetic to them. Indeed, one of the reasons EPA often tried to make regulatory compromises that would lead to voluntary compliance on the part of industry was that the agency was often given a very rough time by federal district judges when it filed local suits seeking to compel industries to comply.

The split between the D.C. Circuit and the district courts was a natural one. The D.C. Circuit usually first saw an agency rule on appeal immediately after its promulgation. Consequently, it first saw the rule in the abstract before its application to any particular facility or locality. At that point arguments about cost and economic disruption appeared speculative. Basically, what the court had to work with were the words of the statute, the agency rule-making record and the words of the rule. Given that costs would be in the future and would be incurred in places far away from Washington, D.C., where the court sat, it is little wonder that the court was usually more impressed with the first two levels of the statute and tended to underplay the fudge factors in the third.

In hearing implementation cases, the district courts were confronted with very immediate and real costs to industry and very real threats of job losses and massive disruptions in the economic life, not of some far away place, but of the places where the judges lived. In many respects a federal district judge is the closest thing to a dictator that we tolerate in our political system. No one elected them in the first place, and they hold office for life. Unlike the circuit courts, where judges serve in panels of three or more and are at least restrained by one another, district judges sit alone. In their own court rooms, they are little tin gods whom no one ever dares contradict. This godlike isolation and independence is a major factor accounting for the persistence of some district judges in pushing highly unpopular policies against massive resistance, such as bussing remedies in school desegregation cases. Nevertheless, a Pittsburgh district judge faced with the prospect of shutting down Pittsburgh right now is more likely to hesitate than a Washington judge told that his decision might shut down Pittsburgh later. During this hesitation, and amidst pleas that various exceptions and qualifications be taken into account, the third level of the statutes tended to loom larger in the minds of district judges than of Washington judges.

The period of the sixties and seventies was not a great hymn to regulation entirely without discords or countermelodies. Nevertheless, it did represent a relatively whole-hearted commitment to high levels of regulation by all three branches of government. Dominated by a young Democratic majority, Congress often took the lead in producing the new legislation. Republican presidents were sometimes less enthusiastic, but they too not only went along but appointed committed regulatory leaders.

Perhaps the most remarkable role was played by the courts. In New Deal days, courts expressed their support of agency regulation by staying out of the agencies' way. In the sixties and seventies, the most important of the regulatory courts, the D.C. Circuit, expressed that support by emphasizing the technology- and agency-forcing provisions of the new statutes and insisting that the agencies do a superpluralist and then synoptic job of enforcing them.

In a sense, the Circuit was acting at cross purposes. Its constant multiplication of procedural demands on the agencies tended to slow down their rule-making even as the court applauded their vigorous action. At the same time, the very high level of court involvement tended to strengthen the hands of the litigation sections within the agencies, sections that wanted to push vigorous action and often seemed most comfortable when they achieved a confrontational stance toward the regulated. Moreover, the agencies began to learn how to cope with the new judicial demands for full scale rule-making records that presented at least the appearance of synopticism. As they learned, they began to win judicial approval of most of their rules even if it took longer to make them. Given the almost complete inaction of the Supreme Court in this area for many years, the agencies and the D.C. Circuit formed a proregulatory alliance that added a final touch of judicial legitimacy to the regulatory vigor of Congress and the agencies.

Deregulation

Sometime in the seventies, the green began to fade a little in American public life. The magnitude of this fading should not be overemphasized, and attempting to account for changes in public sentiment always involves more speculation than science. In part, there was a general loss of confidence in government throughout the Western democratic social-welfare nations during the late seventies and early eighties. Long periods of Socialist rule in a number of European countries were interrupted. In the United States Jimmy Carter and Ronald Reagan each became president by running against "Washington." Even incumbent congressmen often ran against Congress in their bids for reelection. Much of this unrest had no direct link to regulation. It seemed to arise largely from the increased perception that more and more government spending on social welfare programs did not seem to make people happier and happier or to end poverty.

One aspect of this general unrest did seem to be more closely linked to regulation. During the sixties, it was rather widely assumed that American and Western European economies had reached such high levels of productivity that they no longer needed to concern themselves primarily with further economic growth. They could tolerate some cutback in growth rates and even some reduction in overall production in order to achieve a cleaner, safer, healthier environment. We all appeared to have more than enough cars and refrigerators and TV sets. What we needed was more clean air and open space. We could easily absorb the costs of environmental improvement without really cutting into our standard of living. In the eighties, it suddenly became far less clear that the industrialized nations of the West were so rich and so far ahead of everybody else that they could shift radically from economic growth to improving the quality of life. We began worrying about the costs of government's regulatory programs as well as its welfare programs.

We have noticed that much of the cost of the new regulatory programs initially appeared acceptable to Congress because those costs were to be borne by the regulated, not the taxpayers. Once Americans began to worry about the national economy as a whole, however, this appearance of cost shifting disappeared. In the sixties, it was we, the people or the public or the consumers against them, the polluters or big business or special interests. We would get the benefits, and they would pay the costs. In the eighties, it became we, the American economy against the economies of the rest of the world with the fear that industrial production and jobs and money would shift abroad, threatening the living standards of all Americans. If environmental and safety regulation made American products more costly, discouraged investment, and threatened economic growth, then we, the Americans paid the cost and they, the

Japanese and the Koreans and the Germans benefited. In the sixties, we worried about saving the environment for our children. Today, we worry about whether they will manage to have a standard of living as high as their parents. Today, the endangered species we may worry about most are the steel worker and the farmer. Government is seen as imposing regulatory costs that must be balanced against regulatory benefits.

A general loss of confidence in government as the solution to all our problems and a general anxiety about national economies occurred throughout the Western world and led to a more critical attitude toward government regulation of the economy. This critical attitude flowered into the "deregulation" movement that has captured so much political support in recent years.[14]

To speak of a deregulation movement is a bit too simple. It disguises the basic fact that while we have been doing away with some regulation of a few industries, the total amount of government regulation has continued to increase. Indeed, even the Reagan administration can only brag that it has decreased the rate at which new regulations are enacted, not that it has decreased the total amount of regulation.

One way to unravel this complexity is to distinguish between old and new regulation. We have seen that a kind of corollary of capture theory was a life-cycle model. As agencies got older, they lost their early regulatory vigor and became more subject to capture. It also just so happened that the older regulatory agencies were single-industry regulators and thus more likely to acquire a certain sympathy for the industry regulated than the newer all-industry agencies such as OSHA and EPA. Much of the deregulation movement has been aimed at the old single-industry regulators and has been occurring at a time when there is still considerable enthusiasm for the new health, safety, and environmental regulation. Thus an apparent paradox of more regulation and less regulation is resolved in part into an off-with-the-old, on-with-the-new phenomenon.

The moves to deregulate long-haul trucking, radio, airlines, and natural gas, and to reduce regulation of railroads, banking, and television are largely built around a common rationale. Many years ago, Congress was confronted by quasi-natural monopolies or situations where a small number of operators with reduced competition appeared to be desirable even if not inevitable. In response, Congress passed regulatory legislation that legitimated the quasi-monopoly but substituted regulatory controls in the public interest for the market place controls that would have operated had the industry been more competitive.

Over time, however, these regulatory controls had come to serve the public badly for a number of reasons. In some instances, agencies had been captured and their regulations had come to favor the industry against the public. In others, the regulations had been well-intended but turned out to be wrong. They led to inefficient investment and the unwarranted cross-subsidization of some classes of customers or industries or parts of the country by others. In other instances yet, economic or technological changes had ended the necessity or desirability of a particular quasi-monopoly. It would have been replaced by healthy and economically efficient competition but for the legal regimes of regulation that were needlessly preserving monopoly.

It is not clear that deregulators were always correct in their analysis or solely devoted to serving the public good as opposed to the interests of specific sectors of the economy. Nevertheless, their common claim was that certain bodies of regulation were artificially maintaining monopolies where free competition would yield better results. Merely by sweeping away the regulation, the public good would be better served.

This facet of deregulation accounts for some political phenomena that might otherwise have appeared rather strange. In Congress, deregulation often brought together liberals and conservatives at the very time when the same liberals continued to champion newer forms of regulation. It permitted liberal Democrats associated in the public mind with now disreputable "big government" to show that they too were against big government. And it tended to render defenseless even the spokesmen of those big industries that really, deep down would have preferred to remain regulated. After all, they had been among the most prominent critics of such regulation in the past.

Until the Reagan administration, the deregulation campaign

had moved chiefly against segments of the old regulation. Gradually, however, attacks began to mount against the new regulation as well. They came largely, but not entirely, from Republican and conservative sources.

The problem began, in a sense, in the earliest days of OSHA, which started off with an extremely mechanical mode of safety enforcement. It instructed its inspectors to cite every violation no matter how minor, and it wrote many of its own regulations in extremely rigid ways. Tales were soon rife of OSHA inspectors insisting that every fire extinguisher in a huge plant be moved six inches because OSHA regulations required that they be mounted three feet above the floor and the plant's were two feet six inches. If the change was not made, the inspector would issue six hundred citations each time he visited the plant, one for each extinguisher. OSHA soon engendered a considerable spirit of resistance in the private sector which, finding it could not reason with the inspectors, took to fighting out a high proportion of the citations in court.[15]

OSHA's problems served as a kind of prelude to the increased worries about the new regulation that almost necessarily followed from the shift in public concerns that occurred in the 1980s. If there is a general concern about "big government" and about maintaining an efficient economy with a substantial rate of growth, the new regulation cannot go entirely unscathed.

The attacks on the new regulation did not take the form of questioning its basic values of health, safety and environmental purity. Those retained a strong hold on the minds of most Americans. Instead they came in the form of questioning the efficiency of the new regulations and of counterbalancing another value, economic prosperity, against the new regulatory values.

Regulatory Analysis

The efficiency arguments came in a number of forms. One form attached itself to a long tradition of public administration that we have encountered before. Stretching back to the Federalists, we have the tradition that government business, like all business, should be run in a businesslike way. Out of this tradition grew the Budget and Accounting Act of 1921 and a whole host of subsequent attempts to impose scientific budgeting on government. These have included "line-item" and "zero-based" budgeting, "cost-benefit analysis," and the "systems analysis" that was first introduced in the defense area and spread to the rest of government. All of these were methods for assuring that government knew exactly how much it was spending on each of its programs and activities and how much value it was getting for each dollar spent.[16]

The environmental movement itself took advantage of this scientific budgeting tradition when it invented the idea of the "environmental impact statement." The Environmental Protection Act requires that the government not take any proposed action that might affect the environment until it has completed an environmental impact statement. Such a statement is a form of cost-benefit analysis in which not only the monetary costs to the government but the anticipated environmental costs of a government program are weighed against its anticipated benefits. Environmentalists have used the environmental impact statement requirement as a weapon to delay projects they wanted to block. They have also used it as a means of inserting environmental experts into the government agencies where they can speak more effectively for environmental values. Nonetheless, such statements take the ostensible form of rational budgeting. They require the government to take into account a set of very real costs that it had not taken into account before because they do not occur as direct, out-of-pocket money costs to the Treasury. Like most rational budgeting devices, the environmental impact statement is a species of synopticism. It requires the agency to consider all costs and alternatives so as to achieve its goal at the least cost to the environment or at that cost which accurately reflects the relative priority of environmental value among the several priorities being pursued by the agency.

For those concerned about the cost in economic disruption, shutdowns, job losses, and reduced rates of economic growth that might occur as a result of the new health, safety, and environmental regulation, the environmental impact statement had one wonderful feature. Remember that part of the attraction of all this legislation to Congress had been that most of its costs would fall upon the private sector and would not become direct, out-of-pocket monetary costs to government. Environmental impact statements required government to treat certain costs directly borne by someone else, namely those who valued the environment, as if they were direct costs to government. They required government to balance those costs against benefits in attempting to justify its actions. So why not also require regulatory impact statements that require that the indirect costs of regulation borne by industry also to be treated as costs which must be balanced against anticipated benefits in justifying proposed agency regulatory actions? If what we are concerned with is the whole national economic environment, then all the costs and benefits to that whole environment of any proposed government action ought to be taken into account.[17]

The demand for regulatory impact statements began among both liberals and conservatives engaged in deregulating the old regulation. It soon spread to those whose real interest was in slowing down the new regulation and particularly in narrowing the goals stated in those statutes. It could provide a way of cutting back on their most devil-may-care technology and agency forcing provisions. Environmentalists had used the environmental impact statement to slow down and cut back on government actions that harmed the environment, even when environmentalists were not strong enough to block those actions entirely, for often such actions served other highly valued goals of the society like flood control, defense, highway transportation, and agriculture. The regulatory impact statement could be used to restrain health, safety, and environmental regulation that could not be directly attacked successfully because health, safety, and environment remained strongly held American values even in the eighties.

The regulatory impact statement changed its name to regulatory analysis.[18] The regulatory analysis movement culminated in the well-known executive order by President Reagan directing that the agencies conduct a cost-benefit analysis of every proposed regulation and submit these analyses for verification to the Office of Management and Budget. Cost-benefit analysis is obviously one aspect of synoptic decision making. In a period in which the courts were already demanding that the agencies make rules synoptically, there could hardly be objections to their chief executive also requiring them to do so and reviewing their efforts.

One major conflict did arise over the move to cost-benefit analysis. To require agencies to do cost-benefit analysis is not quite the same thing as to require them to enact only rules that can be justified under cost-benefit analysis, that is rules whose benefits exceed their costs. But the requirement to do the analysis certainly puts a lot of pressure on agencies to move toward such rules. It is tough for an agency to say to OMB and to the public, "We want this rule even though it costs a lot more than it is worth." Yet the great regulatory statutes of the sixties and seventies, particularly in their first level of sweeping general commands, often seemed to say that workers were entitled to a safe work place and citizens to clean air and water no matter what the cost—even if the costs were higher than the benefits. On the other hand, the third level, fudge-factor language of the same statutes often suggested that costs should be taken into account, that perhaps ten thousand people should not be thrown out of work so that a stream which used to be eighty percent polluted would now only be seventy-six percent polluted.

Regulation at the Margin

Health, safety, and environmental investments are no more subject to the problems that economists label marginality than are other forms of investment. When such investments are mandated by government regulation, however, marginality can come to look particularly dramatic. Let us suppose a textile mill that has been putting eight hundred parts of cotton dust per million parts of air into its work space, an amount that is clearly unhealthy for its workers. It may be able to reduce the dust from eight hundred parts to one hundred parts at a cost of half a million dollars worth of fans and filtering equipment. That cost might be easily justified in terms of the improved health of the workers. There might be little or no observable health benefits in a further reduction from one hundred parts to ten parts of dust per million parts of air. And such a further reduction might be enormously costly, far more costly than the reduction from eight hundred to one hundred. The very biggest fans and finest filters might not work to get those few final microscopic dust bits out of the air of the existing factory. It might be necessary to build a whole new factory with totally redesigned machinery in order to get this last increment of dust reduction.

In this situation, costs are rising dramatically *at the margin*. After we have removed most of the dust, the cost of removing each additional or marginal particle of dust is far higher than was the cost of removing the first particle. The cost of removing the last particle of dust we choose to remove may be thousands of times higher than the cost of removing the first particle just as the time it takes to find the last little bit of a broken glass on the kitchen floor may be a thousand times longer than the time it took to find the first piece of that broken glass. Furthermore, after a certain point observable benefits at the margin tend to drop very sharply as costs rise very sharply. It may be very easy to show that workers who breathe a lot of cotton dust get lung diseases more frequently than those who don't. There may be little or no evidence that workers who breathe tiny amounts do, although the suspicion may remain that if a lot of dust hurts a lot a little must do some harm.

One response by zealous regulators to the margin problem has been the great cancer ploy.[19] We don't know why Americans are so much more concerned with cancer than other people are, but that fear has been put to a number of interesting political uses. The Nixon administration thought of itself as a conservative Republican one bent on reducing the size and scope of government (although in fact it did not accomplish any reduction). In spite of its goals, it wanted to respond somehow to Democratic criticisms that Republicans were entirely negative in their approach, always saying no to the needs and welfare of the American people. So the Nixon administration declared a war on cancer to demonstrate that it wanted to act positively to help the American people. Such a war had a number of virtues. It got a lot of publicity because Americans are so afraid of cancer. And precisely because no cure for cancer was known and existing treatments for cancer were not extraordinarily expensive, it was a cheap war. The cost of increases in government grants for medical and biological research related to cancer was peanuts compared to the costs of most government programs.

In the seventies, those agencies enforcing health, safety, and clean air and water statutes with grandly stated goals and agency- and technology-forcing features quickly hit the margin problem. Offhand it might seem insane to require a company to spend millions to eliminate the very last bit of pollution when the agency could not prove that anyone would be injured in any way if the last bit stayed. One response was the cancer ploy.

Suppose we know that a lot of some pollutant is a carcinogen, a cancer causer. Given how terrible cancer is, shouldn't we get rid of even the smallest bit of that pollutant, even if we don't yet have persuasive evidence that small amounts of it cause cancer and even if it costs an enormous amount to get rid of the last bit? In other words, shouldn't we assume that anything that causes cancer in large doses causes it in small doses too until someone proves otherwise? And if we make such an assumption, shouldn't we be willing to spend any amount necessary to remove the last bit of the carcinogen even if doing so may turn out to save only a very few lives over a very, very long time and at very high costs?

Part of the potency of the cancer ploy is its contact with our understandable reluctance to put a dollar value on human life. Because cancer is a death-dealing disease, those who would argue that it is not worth an extra ten or twelve million dollars to reduce that last speck of something that may be a carcinogen are "putting a price on human life" or saying that a life is not worth ten or twelve million dollars. So opposing those who want to incur enormous marginal costs in order to achieve small and uncertain benefits is a very uncomfortable position in which to be. Once cancer was invoked, pointing to the enormous marginality problems of regulation became down right un-American. It was the litigation sections of the agencies that particularly nurtured the cancer ploy. It appeared to be a dandy way of getting judges to focus exclusively on the grand language of the statutes and give short shrift to the statutory language that suggested that some attention be paid to costs.

What we have been describing is a confrontation between increasing demands for cost-benefit, "rational," synoptic decision-making by government and the continuing commitment to health, safety, and the purity of the environment at any cost.[20] This confrontation came to a head in a number of cases, the most famous of which are worth discussing briefly because they illustrate the problem and the judicial response to it.

In attempting to write a standard for permissible levels of benzine in work environments, OSHA found that exposure to benzine created a measurable risk of cancer. However, at the time, researchers were unable to calculate a dose-response curve for low levels of exposure. They did not know how many, if any, cancers would result from prolonged exposures to low levels of benzine. OSHA took the position that where a pollutant was a known carcinogen at high levels of exposure, low levels of exposure should also be banned unless it could be proven that they posed no cancer risk. It set the permissible level at the lowest level its instruments could measure. Industry made the classic marginality argument in response. It cost more and more to get out less and less benzine as you moved from high levels to very low levels, and there was no direct evidence that movement from low to very low levels resulted in any health benefit.

This case[21] presented the Supreme Court with a dilemma. The OSHA statute contained sweeping language guaranteeing workers a safe work place. It did not contain a specific provision requiring that cost-benefit analysis be done or that the benzine standard set by the agency be shown to yield more benefits than costs. Yet the Court did not want to read the statute as insisting that perfect air cleanliness be attained in factories, no matter how high the costs, even if no health benefit could be demonstrated for the removal of the very last traces of pollutants. In other words the Court did not think that Congress had wanted to entirely dismiss the marginality problem.

The Court concluded that OSHA must first pass a threshold requirement of showing that a particular level of pollution constituted a "significant risk" to health. Only then could it forbid that level of pollution. The "significant risk" standard was a kind of minimum cost-benefit analysis. OSHA could not impose regulatory costs unless it could show that a "significant" benefit could result.

In a subsequent case,[22] other industries argued that OSHA was required by the statute to enact only standards that met complete cost-benefit criteria—that not only yielded "significant" benefits but benefits higher than the costs of achieving them. The Supreme Court rejected this reading of the statute, holding that Congress had chosen to require more health protection for workers than could have been justified in cost-benefit terms. The Court said Congress was entitled to decide that health benefits to workers were more important than the cost to industry of attaining them. So the Court stuck to the minimum "significant risk" cost-benefit constraint on OSHA.

The result has been about the same for the other new regulatory programs. So, with some exceptions, regulatory agencies now do cost-benefit analyses of each proposed rule and submit these analyses to the president's Office of Management and Budget for review. Usually, however, they are under no legal constraint to limit their rules to those that can be justified by cost-benefit analysis. Indeed, the refusal of an agency to set a particular standard only because it does not yield more benefits than costs usually will be held by a court to violate the agency's statute if the proposed rule can be shown to yield some benefits. The courts have generally been moving toward a balancing approach under which they expect the agencies to take some account of economic costs. Regulation may be pushed so far that some plants are shut down but not so far as to shut down a substantial percent of the capacity of an industry.[23]

As things currently stand, deregulatory schools of thought have dramatized the problem of marginal costs and benefits and have introduced cost-benefit analysis. They have not, however, overcome the regulatory vitality of the sixties and seventies that treated health, safety, and environmental benefits as so important that they must be attained even at costs that are far higher than would be justified by straight economic calculation.

What we have seen, then, is that in the eighties, widespread unease with "big government," the deregulation movement in general, and increased sensitivity to the costs of regulation have all touched the new regulatory statutes and agencies of the sixties and seventies. Nevertheless, the commitment to vigorous enforcement of these regulations has remained firm, not only in liberal political circles but in the general population. Even the conservative political forces of the Reagan administration have retained a public commitment to the new regulations. In these areas they have tended to confine their fervor for deregulation to giving regulatory costs greater weight and seeking to curb what they view as overenthusiastic, too-rapid and economically and technologically unrealistic new rule making. There have also been accusations, particularly in connection with the Environmental Protection Agency, that precisely because the Reagan administration could not openly espouse deregulation in the new regulatory agencies, it simply tried to trash them by appointing agency heads so hostile or so unskilled that they threw their agencies into disarray. Such trashing is hardly a permanent solution.

The deregulators have managed to change the Washington mood toward big government at least slightly and at least for the short run,[24] but the response of the proregulation forces is probably more significant for the issue of judicial control in the long run.

Chapter Five

An Independent Fourth Branch

We have been looking at the deregulation movement because we are trying to show that ideology must be linked with moral and political philosophy, semi-autonomous developments in administrative law itself, and shifts in public attitudes about technocracy in order to understand why lawyers and judges act the way they do. We can look at the new set of themes now emerging in administrative law as ideology. These themes are a set of legal ideas used to defend and legitimate a particular political position in the conflict over deregulation. To understand this ideological aspect of the emerging administrative law, let us put ourselves in the shoes of those who, in the eighties, wish to preserve the regulatory enthusiasms of the sixties and seventies in their full vigor.

From that viewpoint, the prospect of Congress is not so good as it was. Congress has not lost its fundamental commitment to health, safety, and environmental values. When administrative or judicial interpretations appear to have undercut basic provisions of the new regulatory statutes, Congress has replied quickly with amendments that restored the statutes' vigor. Nevertheless, the Congress of the early eighties has been particularly concerned with balancing budgets and reducing taxes, with deficits and the damage done to American enterprise by foreign competition. The old "smokestack" industries like steel are suffering most from foreign competition, and they are precisely the industries under the greatest regulatory pressure. It no longer seems as clear as it once did that we can ignore the costs of regulation because America is so rich that it can afford any level of extra costs, nor does it seem as likely that companies that claim they will have to shut down in the face of new regulatory costs are bluffing.

Given our new concerns with the American economy, Congress is no longer the aggressive champion of the damn-the-torpedoes approach to regulation that it once was. The congressional committees overseeing the new regulatory agencies are the targets of increasing pressure. Industries and local groups concerned with factory closings and job loss point out that American industries which must incur the costs of meeting our high standards are at a disadvantage with foreign competitors. Congress will not roll back the statutes, but neither will it push the agencies very hard to move implementation forward.

If Congress has retired to a neutral corner, the president has become the opponent of those who want to maintain the vigor of the new regulation. President Reagan is front-and-center in the deregulation movement and many of his top appointees have qualified for public office largely by their antibureaucracy, antiregulation stances.

The falling away of Congress and the active antiregulatory posture of the presidency have led to a new concern with the "separation of powers" among those concerned with administrative law and regulation. If you don't trust Congress and know that the president is the enemy, who is left to love and nurture the health, safety and environmental legislation of the sixties and seventies? All that is left is the bureaucracy of the new federal agencies who were recruited only recently and retain their enthusiasm for doing what they were hired to do. They want to regulate in behalf of the great public values of health, safety, and environmental purity. So it becomes attractive to those favoring regulation to turn the federal bureaucracy into an independent branch of government. Such a branch would be free of the president, even free of the Congress of the eighties, but loyal to the sweeping statutory language of the sixties and seventies.

At first glance, the creation of such an independent fourth branch would seem difficult in view of the constitutional place of the president as head of the executive branch and its agencies. It might seem particularly difficult in the light of the New Deal theory of the strong presidency that we looked at earlier. A number of factors make it less difficult than it might seem.

First of all, the New Deal theory of the strong presidency fell into some disrepute with Democrats when they realized that there might be quite a few Republican presidents. It also fell into some disrepute with the public more generally when it was employed by Richard Nixon to defend and obscure his misdeeds.

Secondly the constitutional position of presidents vis-a-vis the agencies of the executive branch which they supposedly lead is much more anomalous than it might appear. If Article II of the Constitution named the executive branch departments such as Treasury and Agriculture, then they would draw their authority directly from Article II and presumably be clearly subordinated to the chief executive also created by Article II, the president. The Constitution, however, barely mentions executive departments. In fact, all executive agencies are created by congressionally enacted statutes. The programs they operate are created, defined, and limited by such statutes. In some sense, the agencies and their staffs are responsible to the president as chief of the executive branch of which they are a part. Their legal authority, however, and the prescriptions for the exercise of that authority are to be found in congressional statutes. The executive agencies have two bosses, not one.

It is far easier to get out from under two bosses with ambiguous and contradictory authority than it is to get out from under one boss with clear authority. We shall return to the precise legal doctrine through which two bosses are turned into none after we look at another major factor paving the way toward an independent bureaucratic fourth branch, the recent actions of the independent third branch, the courts.

We have seen that the courts of the sixties and seventies were emboldened to take on far more active supervision of the agencies as American faith in rule by experts or technocrats waned. We have seen that the form of this increased intervention was the creation by courts, with congressional assistance, of a new body of administrative law. This new body of administrative law at first insisted that the agencies give total access to all groups and then moved on to demand that the agencies act synoptically. The courts imposed these demands largely by creating a large body of new procedural rules and judicial review standards for administrative rule-making proceedings.

The basic plan of the APA was to distinguish between agency adjudication and agency rule making. Agencies were to act like courts when they conducted adjudication, holding oral hearings with formal presentation of evidence on both sides and cross examination. They were to enter final orders that looked like court decisions. These final orders were to be supported solely on the evidentiary record of the hearing and by findings of fact and law of the sort found in judicial opinions. And a reviewing court was to review this trial-type record carefully.

Agencies were not to act like courts in conducting rule makings. The agency was to make its rule by whatever internal decision-making process it chose so long as it gave notice, received comments, and accompanied its published rule with a concise and general statement of basis and purpose. There need be no oral hearing, no cross examination, no record, and no findings. And a reviewing court was to intervene only if the agency had committed lunacy.

The long and short of it is that the courts of the sixties and seventies almost entirely obliterated the distinction between adjudication and rule making and required that agency rule making look just like agency adjudication.[1] We have seen earlier that law has a certain measure of autonomous development. In the United States, judges think they are such truly wonderful people, and courts such truly wonderful places, and litigation such a truly wonderful way of getting at truth and resolving conflict, that their almost instinctive reaction whenever they seek to improve some other part of government's behavior is to require it to act like a court. There is, therefore, a kind of natural pressure in administrative law, which is basically the law of judicial review of agency proceedings, toward making more and more agency behavior court-like.

One way to look at the history of American administrative law from its first great outburst in the 1930s is as a gradual movement toward adjudicializing more and more of what agencies do. In the forties and fifties, agency adjudication was made to look like court adjudication. In the sixties and seventies, agency rule making was made to look court-like. In the eighties, there is increasing interest in making the large residual category of what agencies do, which is not adjudication or rule making and is often called the exercise of "discretion," court-like as well.[2]

Even if one does not see this kind of "progress," a similar point may be made. The 1960s public distrust of bureaucracy and technocracy encouraged judges to watch the agencies more closely and improve their conduct. It was natural for judges to believe that the agencies would do better if they were required to use good procedures. It was equally natural for judges to use judicial procedures as their model of what good procedure would be. Agency adjudication already followed judicial procedure. So the judicial task of the sixties and seventies was to require the agencies to use judicial procedures in rule making as well.[3]

The upshot was that agency rule making came to have a very court-like character. With this in mind we can now return to the liberal regulator's shoes. We can ask again how the friends of regulation can turn two bosses into none—that is, get the regulatory bureaucracies out from under a hostile president and a Congress increasingly worried about economic development.

Once we have seen how court-like the rule-making behavior of agencies became in the sixties and seventies, the first answer immediately jumps to mind. If it walks like a duck and quacks like a duck, it's a duck. If the agencies hold court-like adjudications and issue court-like opinions, then they are courts, or at least very court-like. And what is one of the most important characteristics of courts? Their independence. According to the Constitution, and as a primary article of American political faith, the courts are an independent third branch of American government, not answerable to Congress or president. So shouldn't the court-like agencies be independent too, an independent fourth branch not answerable to either Congress or president?

Stated so baldly, this all may seem a rather simple minded sleight-of-hand. No matter how much they quack like courts, agencies, unlike courts, are a part of the president's executive branch and are the creation of Congressional statute. It is difficult to convey to a lay audience the cumulative effect on lawyers and law students of watching the agencies act in a judicial manner year after year. Imagine our outrage if, at the end of a court trial, the president of the United States called up the judge and told her how he wanted the case to come out. Let us suppose an agency has held a rule-making proceeding that involved hundreds of hours of testimony and thousands of pages of written submissions. It has listened at length to every interested group and heard the rebuttal of each group to the testimony of every other. It has compiled a thousand-page-long rule-making record. It has then composed a statement showing that it has acted synoptically to consider every significant issue and arrive at the best possible decision. Those who have been watching and participating in such a process are going to be equally outraged if, just before the agency publishes its final rule, the president calls to tell the agency what rule it should adopt. Once the agencies have gone through a highly judicialized procedure, the President is bound to look like an "outsider" trying to intervene unfairly.[4]

About the same thing happens to Congress. To be sure, we have to begin by remembering that when an agency makes a rule, it is actually exercising a part of Congress' law making power delegated to it by congressional statute. No one denies that if Congress does not like a rule that an agency has made under a particular statute, Congress may amend the statute to change the rule. If Congress passed a no-vehicle-in-wildernesses statute, and the agency made a no-horse-drawn-sled rule, Congress may amend the statute to read "no vehicles except horse-drawn sleds." Of course, Congress may do the same thing to courts. If Congress does not like the interpretation that courts have been giving a certain statute, Congress may amend it to make clear that it means something other than what the judges have been saying it means. Nevertheless, we would not want Congress calling a judge on the phone to tell him how it wanted a statute interpreted in a particular case that the judge was hearing. So, short of amending the statute, Congress begins to look like an outsider, too, if it "interferes" with a highly judicialized rule-making proceeding.

By the 1950s, it had begun to occur to Congress that delegating huge amounts of its law-making authority to the agencies and then controlling the exercise of that delegated power only by Congress's power to amend the basic statute was not entirely satisfactory. Congress is not set up to enact statutes or amendments to statutes quickly. Indeed, its whole organization and procedures make law making far more difficult for Congress than rule making is for the agencies, even under the elaborate rule-making procedures imposed on the agencies by the courts in the sixties and seventies. And there are many agencies, but only one Congress. The agencies make many more rules each year than Congress makes statutes. It would be difficult for even a fast-moving Congress to amend enough of its statutes quickly enough to actually closely supervise agency rule making in this way. It is nigh on to impossible given the legislative inertia built into Congress.

For this reason Congress began attaching a new device to its statutes delegating law-making power to agencies. It was called the "legislative veto." There were a lot of different kinds of vetoes. Some provided that, once an agency had made a rule, it did not become law until both houses of Congress had approved it within a certain time period. Others provided that a rule became law unless both houses had disapproved it. Or it became law only after a particular committee of one house or both houses had approved it. Or it did not become law if a committee or both committees had disapproved it. So there were one-house and two-house vetoes. There were committee vetoes as opposed to vetoes requiring action by the whole House or

Senate. There were vetoes in which a rule went into effect unless Congress or some part of it intervened actively to stop the rule and vetoes in which the rule would not go into effect unless Congress or some part of it approved the rule.

Obviously, some forms of the veto created the potential for active and detailed congressional review of rule making and others really only allowed Congress to intervene if the agency's rule was totally out of bounds. Where a committee veto was provided it was wielded by the committee that engaged in continuous oversight of the agency. For instance, the House Agriculture Committee would exercise the veto over the Forestry Service of the Department of Agriculture. So a one-house committee veto gave a lot of extra punch to a committee that knew enough and might care enough to use it often.

Where a rule came into force unless both houses passed resolutions vetoing it within thirty days of its issuance by the agency, there was actually little opportunity for congressional supervision. Only if a rule rubbed many people the wrong way would it gain enough adverse attention to overcome legislative inertia and bring resolutions to a vote. So Congress gave itself some control over rule making. It also specified just about how much control over each kind of rule making it wanted by enacting different veto provisions for different rules.

For those who wished to create a proregulatory independent fourth branch of government, the legislative veto was anathema because it provided for congressional control of agency rule making. We saw earlier that the New Deal theory of the strong presidency was taken over by President Nixon. In spite of the disastrous results of that theory in Nixon's hands, it has stuck with Republicans when they hold the presidency. Many conservative supporters of the strong Republican presidency have opposed the legislative veto because they don't understand what is really going on in regulatory politics. They have reasoned that if the legislative veto strengthens congressional control over the bureaucracy, it must weaken presidential control over it. They have not understood that the aim of liberal regulators has been to break control by both Congress and the president. Conservative antiregulators should be worried, not about congressional versus presidential control, but about any control over the bureaucracy versus no control.

As a result of this curious mistake by conservatives, the legislative veto was attacked by a strange alliance of Reaganites and the very "public interest" law firms in Washington that constantly used the courts to block the administration's deregulation policies.[5] The Supreme Court gave this alliance a great victory, declaring the legislative veto device unconstitutional[6] on a theory of separation of powers. The Court's theory was so simplistic and naive that it had disappeared even from high school textbooks, but only some time after these rather elderly judges had finished high school.[7] So great progress was made in getting rid of Congress, the second boss.

Statutory Duty

We have seen that the growth of court-like conduct in agency rule making increasingly made the president look like an outsider whose intervention would seem unfair. Congress was now denied the right to provide by statute for its own intervention through the legislative veto and so also became an outsider. If a phone call from the president to a judge deciding a case is outrageous so is a phone call from a congressman or a congressional committee. So informed congressional "pressure" on agency rule making also increasingly came to seem wrong.

In spite of these victories by the proregulators, however, the two bosses still seemed to exercise enough control to threaten the vigor of regulation. The president could appoint agency heads who were not enthusiastic about regulation. By requiring so much synopticism (e.g., cost-benefit analysis) in the rule-making process that it would take forever to make a new rule, the president might stall the rule-making process. By not seeking to appropriate much money for the regulatory agencies and not pressing the agencies to enforce vigorously, Congress, and particularly the committees that oversaw the regulatory agencies, might cooperate in this stall.

What was needed was a theory that would preserve the regulatory vigor of the sixties and seventies, the enthusiasm that existed for the statutes when they were first passed, into the eighties when they were very much less the fair-haired children of American politics. And the theory had to be a legal theory, one which would allow proregulators to use courts to force agencies to get back to vigorous regulation in spite of presidential hostility and congressional inattention.

The needed theory is the theory of statutory duty or statutory right.[8] It can be called either *duty* or *right* because if an agency has a legal duty to do something, some individual probably has a right to have that thing done. If the OSHA statute commands OSHA to insure that workers have a safe workplace, then OSHA has a duty to make workplaces safe and workers have a right to a safe workplace. Or at least they have a right to OSHA's best efforts to get them one. This correlative or reciprocal relation of duties and rights is important ideologically. Most of the statutes involved tell the agencies to regulate rather than explicitly creating individual legal rights. When someone complains that the government has not been doing something it is supposed to do, most Americans are not likely to be terribly upset. If someone complains that his rights have been violated by the government, then our juices begin to flow. So those interested in preserving regulatory enthusiasm are likely to stir a lot of rights language into the statutory duty theory.[9]

This introduction of individual rights language into statutes that are really about regulation is further facilitated by a special feature of much of the sixties and seventies legislation. Those statutes were passed at the time when people were trying to cure the pathologies of pluralism with more pluralism, that is, by granting more and more complete group access so that all groups would have truly equal access. As we have seen, it was also a time of fear of agency capture by the regulated and therefore of a search for devices to force the agencies into regulatory action. One device that was thought to accomplish both group equalization and agency forcing was to grant all groups and individuals very easy access to the courts so that they could sue government agencies that were not implementing the law. So most of the new statutes contained very generous standing provisions. Where an agency has a legal duty to do something, but no individual may sue it to force it to do its legal duty, it is hard to assert that the government's duty is also an individual right. For we often think of a legal right as something an individual can get enforced by a court. Where a statute appears to impose legal duties on agencies and also gives individuals maximum opportunities to get into court about them, it is much easier to think about the whole thing in terms of individual rights.[10]

Returning, however, to the basic concept of statutory duty, we will be able to see very quickly that it is an attempt to resolve the two-bosses paradox of separation of powers that we noted earlier in a way that will carve out an independent bureaucracy wedded to vigorous regulation.

We have seen that the Administrative Procedures Act divided agency behavior up into adjudication, rule making, and discretion. But what about the agency decision to adjudicate? That decision typically took the form of issuing a complaint against some individual or company charging that it had violated some agency regulation. The agency then conducted an adjudication and pronounced guilt or innocence of the charge it had made. So the agency action in either starting or not starting an adjudication looked very much like what prosecutors do in criminal law. Traditionally the decision of a prosecutor either to prosecute or not to prosecute an individual whose possible wrongdoing is brought to his or her attention has been viewed as a purely discretionary one. So when an agency decides not to conduct an adjudication, that will normally be viewed as an act of agency discretion comparable to prosecutorial discretion.

As long as rule making was viewed as quasi-legislative, that is as like law making by Congress, the decision of an agency to make a rule or not make a rule also looked like a purely discretionary one. We never say that Congress has a duty to pass a particular law or indeed any laws at all. So an agency exercising Congress's delegated law-making powers had no such duty either.

Of course if the agency did make a rule, that rule had to be in harmony with the statute that the rule was supposed to implement. It was supposed to observe whatever limits and conditions Congress placed on its delegation of rule-making power to the agency. The APA commands courts to strike down "unlawful" agency rules as well as "arbitrary and capricious" ones. In this sense, agencies always had statutory duties. If they made a rule at all, they had a duty to make one that followed the mandate to the agency laid down in the statute. On the other hand, if the agency chose not to make a rule at all, wasn't it doing just what Congress did when it chose not to enact a new law?

We have seen that the courts gradually moved us from a vision of rule making as quasi-legislative to one of rule making as quasi-judicial by requiring all kinds of new adjudicatory style procedures in rule making. That, of course, would not change our view of the decision to make or not make a rule as a discretionary one. For if agency rule making came to look like agency adjudication, then we would simply begin to think of the decision to begin a rule making as like the decision to begin an adjudication, that is, as like prosecutorial discretion.

So under either legislative or adjudicative analogies, an agency decision to make or not make a rule seemed to be a purely discretionary one and so not reviewable at all by courts according to the APA. Moreover, there is an extremely practical problem that seems very, very dramatic to judges who are asked to order an agency to make a rule. Judges don't like to order Congress or state legislatures to make laws because if they disobey, judges don't want to face ordering a whole legislature off to jail for contempt. Of course, a judge wouldn't be overjoyed to order the head of EPA or the Secretary of Agriculture off to jail either. If push came to shove, however, the judge could do so without assaulting the whole of one of the three great branches of a sovereign government. The practical problem that judges confront in commanding an agency to make a rule is of an entirely different kind. It is certainly possible for a court to make such an order and to threaten to jail agency heads if it is not obeyed. But how do you command an agency to make a good rule?

We have seen that the courts themselves have piled more and more procedural requirements on rule making and capped them by requiring synoptic rule making, a perfect rule-making process resulting in a substantially correct rule. It takes a great deal of time and careful effort these days for an agency to make a rule that will survive judicial review even when the agency desperately wants to make such a rule. An agency ordered by a court to make a rule it doesn't want to make will have little difficulty making enough mistakes in making the rule so that it will not survive judicial review. So a court will be very reluctant to order an agency to make a rule. Such an order is too easily sabotaged.

A number of circumstances have combined, however, to render the doctrine of positive statutory duty to make rules more feasible than it would at first appear, both theoretically and practically. First of all, a lot of people want such a theory to become law. The Reagan deregulators have not been able to mount a frontal assault on the health, safety, and environmental regulations of the sixties and seventies. Neither Congress nor the voters are in a mood to repeal them although they may be less enthusiastic about damn-the-torpedoes enforcement than they were. As a result, the Reaganites frequently try to abate the full impact of these laws by dragging their feet in making the rules necessary to enforce them. Those seeking to maintain the regulatory vigor of these statutes want very badly to be able to force the agencies to act. So they push the statutory-duty theory very hard.

Secondly, we have seen that precisely because Congress distrusted the agencies, the new statutes contained very generous standing provisions so that nearly anyone who wants to can sue the agencies. The APA specifically says that agency inactions as well as actions are reviewable. So nearly anyone who wants an agency to make a rule can at least get into court to push the statutory duty theory. Or, as it was often put, the new statutes had vested rights to a safe workplace, etc., in individuals. The failure of the agency to act constituted a violation of these rights. Surely an individual ought to be able to get a court to order the agency to stop violating his or her rights—that is, to order the agency to make a rule protecting those rights.

Thirdly, one variety of agency-forcing provision Congress put in some of these statutes is a rule-making timetable with fixed deadlines. Not often, but sometimes, the statute specifically required an agency to make a certain rule, for instance on auto exhaust emissions, by a certain date. Rule making may look discretionary in theory because it is quasi-legislative or quasi-prosecutorial. In practice, it may be very difficult to enforce a court order to an agency to make a rule. Nonetheless, a court confronted by an agency that has disobeyed a specific statutory order to make a rule by a certain date would be hard put not to order the agency to obey the law. Most of the instances in which courts have actually used the statutory duty theory to order rule making have involved specific statutory deadlines.

Fourthly, because of the high level of litigation, courts inevitably get a few cases where the practical difficulties of ordering an agency to make a rule are mitigated. The agency may have its rule making all finished, have produced a good rule and then refused to issue it. So ordering it to issue a rule may be ordering it to publish the rule it has already done a good job making.[11] Or the agency may be attempting to rescind an old rule. A court may say, "You either have to make a new rule or keep the old one."[12] Such an order may be tantamount to ordering a new rule because the agency is so unhappy with the old one it can't live with it. It will have to try its best to make a good new one. There have been enough such cases to bring to life a doctrine of a court-enforceable order to make a rule.[13] A doctrine that arises from special circumstances in special cases may be nurtured into a general rule for all cases by lawyers and judges who like it enough.

Finally, the basic notion of statutory duty, that agencies must do what their statutes tell them to do, is hardly deniable. Courts have always reviewed the rules the agencies did make to see whether they contained violations of law. So the notion of an agency's duty to act lawfully has never been in doubt. The doctrine of statutory duty is most dramatic when claimed in its positive form—that courts may order agencies to make rules. It is more often stated, and more often effective in getting the bureaucracy out from under both Congress and the president, when stated in its negative form—that courts should strike down rules that agencies have made when those rules do not conform to the duties laid upon the agencies by statutes.

Statutory Duty and Regulatory Purpose

What characterizes the contemporary push toward statutory duty in this negative form is a little difficult to explain without descending into some of the most technical aspects of administrative law. At the risk of great oversimplification, the new doctrine can be said to be a shift from "reasonableness" to purpose review. Sometimes courts say that where Congress has delegated law-making authority to an agency, the question for the court is only whether, in the light of the statutory language, a reasonable person could have come up with the rule the agency did. At other times courts say that even when Congress has delegated rule making to the agency, the court must determine precisely what the purpose of the statute is and then determine whether the rule fits the legislative purpose. In part, the difference is one of emphasis. In part, however, the issue is whether the court will let the agency itself decide what the purpose of the statute is and then write its rule in the light of the agency's own view of statutory purpose. Some courts are anxious to do their own reading of the statute and make sure that the rule fits what the judges, not the agency, have determined the purpose of the statute to be.

It is the latter approach that is basic to building a statutory duty approach, that is, to judges commanding agencies to fulfill their statutory duty. For simply to tell an agency that it must obey its own version of what the statute says, invented to justify its own rule, is not really to impose any duty on it. It need only hire a couple more lawyers to deliver to it the interpretations it wants. To the degree that courts do their own statutory interpretations, they further the new statutory duty approach. They decide what purpose or duty the statute has laid upon the agency and they command the agency to do it.

The Supreme Court has been notorious for maintaining two lines of precedent on statutory interpretation. One indicates that where a statute delegates rule-making authority to an agency, the courts should defer to the agency's interpretation of its own statute. The other indicates that questions of statutory interpretation are precisely the kinds of questions of law that courts ought to answer for themselves.[14]

If courts were to defer to the interpretation of the sixties and seventies statutes by agencies controlled by the deregulators of the eighties, deregulation would be facilitated. The eighties agencies would issue new rules embodying new interpretations of those statutes which emphasized their third-level fudge factors and treated their first-level commands as mere aspirations. Similarly, the agencies could interpret away many of the second-level agency and technology-forcing provisions of the statutes.

If, on the other hand, courts should not defer to agency interpretations but make their own independent interpretations, and demand that agencies act with fidelity to the statutes as the courts have independently interpreted them,[15] the regulatory vigor of the sixties and seventies statutes *might* be preserved. I say "might" because it would depend on what kind of interpretation the courts made. Those interested in building up a theory of statutory duty in order to create an independent fourth branch, dedicated to vigorous regulation, not only urge courts to do their own interpretation but have a particular style of statutory interpretation in mind.

In their version, courts should not view a congressional statute as a mere summation of group preferences and a recording of group wins and losses in the legislative struggle. Instead, courts should give emphasis to the general public purposes and public values that the statutes incorporate. Of course when a statute commands in very clear language that the interests of a particular group be served, the courts have no choice but to obey. When statutory language will permit of a more public-regarding interpretation and/or when the statutory language is opaque, vague, ambiguous, or internally contradictory, then the courts should interpret that language to further public values.[16]

Such a judicial approach to statutory interpretation is closely allied to the substantive judicial review of agency action that occurs when courts move from incremental to synoptic standards. The courts will decide, not whether the agency has arrived at *a* correct interpretation of the statute, but whether it has arrived at *the* correct interpretation of the statute.[17] And there is likely to be some confusion and overlap between what public policies the judge thinks are best and what public policies he sees as commanded by the statutory language properly interpreted.[18]

A style of statutory interpretation that favors "public regarding," or "public interest," or "public values" interpretations over those that register the concrete claims of particular groups when a statute is ambiguous is obviously tailored to yield a particular outcome for the health, safety, and environmental statutes of the sixties and seventies. It says fairly clearly: save the big regulation commands of level one of these statutes from the quibbles and fudge factors won by particular groups that compose level three.

Indeed, this style of statutory interpretation is likely to lead courts to impose a priority of values on statutes that contain multiple conflicting values. How else could a court come up with a correct, public-regarding interpretation of a statute that was created by a political process that gave each of a number of groups with different values some victories. In order to reach *the* correct interpretation, a court must pretend that Congress has made a choice as to which values incorporated into the statute have priority and what the trade-offs between them must be.[19] Here again, if a court must choose top values for the environmental and health statutes, it will clearly choose level-one values of health and environmental purity rather than level-three values of economic development.

A court-proclaimed and -enforced agency statutory duty to pursue damn-the-torpedos environmental and safety values can effectively armor proregulatory interests against the president and against any attempt at coordinated policy development that refuses to give absolute priority to court-announced statutory purposes.[20]

All these factors combined to create a fairly strong statutory duty doctrine that would direct courts both to order agencies to make rules and to insure that the rules they have made are in accord with the statutory purpose. If the courts could be persuaded to see the purposes of regulatory statutes of the 1960s and 1970s as set exclusively by their general and agency and technology-forcing clauses and not by their various third-level fudge factors and concerns about costs and feasibility, the task of the proponents of vigorous regulation would be completed. The bureaucrats in the agencies who wanted to continue sixties- and seventies-style regulation would be able to assert this statutory duty to the legislative purposes of the sixties and seventies. This assertion could be used as a shield against deregulation attempts by a 1980s president or even Congress, short of major amendments to the statutes. The spirit of the sixties and seventies would be preserved in the eighties and protected from outsiders by a bureaucracy rendered independent of the president and Congress by judicial demands that it do its statutory duty.

Agencies and Courts

The bureaucracy may well have been rendered independent of president and Congress, but it will not really become an independent fourth branch. It will become the total dependent of the courts which define its statutory duties. And those courts may well fill up with Reagan-appointed deregulators who will not read the statutes as having such damn-the-torpedoes purposes. There is no doubt that the statutory duty approach is, for this reason, a far from perfect one for proregulatory forces bent on creating an independent bureaucracy.

It is, nevertheless, better than it might look at first glance. No matter who appointed them or what their personal preferences, judges are going to feel some obligation to maintain continuity of meaning in the statutory law. Certainly they are going to feel far more obligation than are agency heads appointed by a president who opposes the laws and was elected many years after the laws were enacted. Any judge is going to preserve more of the original regulatory vigor of the sixties and seventies statutes than are agency heads who have been chosen for their dedication to undercutting those statutes.

Within the agencies themselves, the politically appointed heads have most power over general interpretations of statutes and least power over compiling and presenting the technical data to support the rules. The long-term career technical bureaucrats in the agencies have most control over the technical support. If the courts substitute their own interpretation of the statute for those of the agency heads, and at the same time demand technologically complete and correct decision making, then they shift the balance of power within agencies from the political heads who oppose regulation to the long-term bureaucrats whose job is regulation.

The political struggle over deregulation has created an ideological agenda for administrative law. Proregulatory forces have been seeking a way to preserve the vigor of health, safety, and environmental regulation against deregulatory forces. To do so they have attempted to create the legal basis for an independent bureaucratic regulatory fourth branch free from presidential intervention and congressional caution. That basis is an emphasis on the agency's duty to achieve the statutory purpose. In the process, they made questions of statutory interpretation crucial to judicial review of administrative action. Particularly emphasized was the problem of judicial commands to agencies to make rules.

We have seen, then, that a number of intellectual movements have led us to our current condition. Philosophers are moving to the view that there are right and wrong government policies, above and beyond the mere summation of individual preferences. Political scientists have found deep flaws in pluralist theories of public administration and law making. At first they sought to cure these flaws by more pluralism and then they began to believe that government might pursue a public interest or common good above and beyond the mere summation of group preferences. Judges have shared the growing popular distrust of technocracy. They have increasingly seen their role as that of policing technocrats from the viewpoint of the layman. At first they sought to correct technocratic pathologies by infusing agency decision making with pluralist participation. They advanced to demanding that bureaucrats act synoptically to reach the good decisions in the public interest that philosophers and political theorists were beginning to say were possible.

All of this was consonant with just the development of administrative law that one would expect from lawyers and judges. Inventing procedural rules is the name of their game. Agency adjudication was put under elaborate court-like rules. Then the lawyers moved on to make procedural rules for agency rule making. At first they were guided by the pluralists and made procedures to insure group access. Then they began to be influenced by our increasing desire that government decisions be guided by values and be rational in the sense of taking costs and benefits fully into account. Almost without realizing what they were doing, lawyers and judges shifted us from pluralist, incremental rule making to synoptic rule making.

In doing so, again almost unconsciously, they moved us from procedural to substantive judicial review of rule making. For pluralist incrementalism says that all a court need do is make sure the procedures are right—that there is enough group access. If the procedures were right, a court doesn't have to look at the substance of the rule at all. Any decision arrived at by full group access must accurately summate group preferences. Any decision that summates group preferences is, according to utilitarian, pluralist ethics, right. When courts added synoptic demands on top of pluralist demands, they were no longer asking only for good rule-making procedures but also for substantively correct rules. Synopticism is about using the right process to arrive at the right decision—the decision that chooses the correct policy to arrive at the true values at the least cost. It entirely merges procedural rightness and substantive rightness.

Another thing that lawyers did when they sought first pluralist perfection and then right answers was to insist that agency rule making look more and more like court adjudication. How could judges be sure that bureaucrats would do good other than by insisting that bureaucrats act like the one set of people that judges knew were good—judges. Or to put this all slightly differently, administrative law sought to limit a larger and larger segment of agency discretion by more and more court-like rules and judicial supervision. Judges demanded that agencies making rules engage in synoptic adjudication.

While all these developments were playing themselves out in philosophy, political and administrative theory, popular attitudes toward technocracy, and in court–agency legal relations, a political battle over regulation and deregulation also raged. The participants naturally used all the ideas and perspectives that were floating around in these other movements as weapons in their own struggle. Proregulatory forces tried to build a picture of a partnership between agencies and courts. In this picture, by both procedural and substantive review, and above all by statutory interpretation, the courts would insist that the health, safety, and environmental bureaucracies established in the sixties and seventies continue in the eighties to make synoptic decisions in a court-like way. These decisions would preserve the regulatory vigor of the sixties and seventies into the eighties. The legal theories propounded would allow the regulators to do so no matter how much other political forces tried to use recently elected members of Congress and presidents to cut back on regulation in the name of economic development.

Chapter Six

The Future of
Judicial Control

What, then, are the new terms of discourse, the words and concepts, which the younger writers and the newer judges are beginning to chew over in the academic writing and the court opinions on administrative law? And what actual changes in the legal and political relations of courts, agencies, legislatures, executives, groups, parties and voters are we likely to see next when we look at the way government agencies make their decisions?

We can start with a clue that we encountered at the very beginning in our look at changes in philosophy and their effect on administrative law. The agencies must "deliberate." Negatively, that means that they must not be captured either by particular interests or by their own special concerns as experts in a particular subject matter. Positively, deliberation includes the whole of pluralist political theory. Agency deliberation must be open. All groups must be invited to participate in it. All interests must be considered.

There may be some disagreement among those pushing deliberation as to the positive role of experts. Obviously, care must be taken so that the professional deformation of experts does not distort deliberation, but hardly anyone proposes that the agencies fire all their technically trained people. Regulation has become more, not less, technically complex over time. We need only think of regulating the nuclear power industry or setting air pollution standards and approving air pollution plans for a large city. So although we are suspicious of them, technicians must either be among the deliberators or close advisors to those who deliberate. Given that deliberation is seen as a kind of open, relatively unstructured discourse among all those concerned enough to want to engage in it, it makes little difference whether one sees the agency experts as "on tap" as advisors or "on top" among the deliberators. In deliberation, the distance between tap and top almost disappears. So an element of technocratic governance as well as the whole of pluralism is incorporated into deliberation.

Is the call for deliberation compatible, however, with administrative law's own movement toward judicialized procedures for rule making? In the eyes of some lawyers it is. Remember that we encountered a "proceduralist" school of law as discourse. The proceduralists think that the "more true" ethical statements and policies that postconsequentialists seek can best emerge from the kind of discourse in which the lawyers for the two sides and the judge engage at a trial. So a trial-like rule-making proceeding would provide an opportunity for the kind of deliberation from which truth will emerge.

Many lawyers, however, are not persuaded that the adversary ritual of the trial is a good framework for deliberation. It may lead to intransigence and overstatement that would appear to be the very opposite of deliberation. And given the large number of interests that perfect pluralism demands participate in rule making, trial-type proceedings become an exceedingly awkward mode of deliberation. Everyone has to have a chance to oppose directly what each of the other parties has to say. That can take forever.[1]

Yet, given the autonomous power of administrative law to go its own way, it does not seem possible at this point to roll back the trial-type procedural requirements that the courts have built up. So there begins to be a movement toward other opportunities for deliberation somehow surrounding the rule-making "trial."[2] At first this movement was largely motivated by the desire to speed up the making and implementation of rules. Adversary rule makings took a very long time if everyone wanted to fight out everything. Their adversary character usually left a number of parties very distinctly unhappy with the rule that resulted, so the losing parties always sought judicial review of the rule. Review delayed the rule's ultimate implementation even longer.

One proposed solution has been mediation before rule making. There has been some success with environmental mediation in which such things as the size and siting of dams has been at issue. The dam builders, local groups, wild river enthusiasts, and other environmentalists have participated in such mediations. Using such mediation as a model, pre-rule-making mediation would seek to get all the interested parties together to cooperate in a nonadversary setting to formulate a draft rule that they could all agree upon. If the agency found the draft satisfactory, it would give notice of it. With agreement already reached, the notice-and-comment proceedings would no longer be adversarial and there would be little incentive to seek subsequent judicial review, so the time it takes to get a rule enunciated and applied would decrease.[3]

There are several major practical problems with mediated rule making that need not concern us here. What is interesting for our purposes is that administrative law scholars and practitioners and their clients are beginning to denigrate adversary procedure and to be attracted by more cooperative modes of discussion and compromise.

There is also some evidence that the fear of capture is decreasing, or to put it a little differently, that the costs of perfect pluralism are now better understood. Expanding the number of parties indefinitely and giving every one an equal say tends to result in undervaluing the contributions of those parties most directly affected. They tend to get lost in the crowd. Suffering from relative neglect and having the most at stake, these groups tend to obstruct the rule implementation process. They seek judicial review of the rules when they are initially announced. Regulated industries in this position also subsequently drag their feet about complying and then resist discrete implementation orders rather than complying voluntarily with the rule.

From the standpoint of deliberation, however, the worst problem created by all the hyperpluralist, access-equalizing, anticapture devices is that they provide very strong incentives to the most knowledgeable parties to limit or falsify their contributions. The industries being regulated know a great deal more about themselves than anyone else does. If there is to be true deliberation about regulating them, they must be major and constant participants in that deliberation. Steps taken to limit industry contacts with agencies in order to guard against agency capture reduce vital industry contributions to deliberation. And steps taken to provide maximum access for groups hostile to the regulated industry, particularly steps that create an adversary process, lead the industries to distort and withhold information so as to make the best case against their adversaries during the agency proceedings and subsequent judicial review. Both those interested in getting faster implementation through voluntary industry compliance and those concerned with the quality of agency deliberation are now beginning to tinker with devices for allowing more continuous and friendly contact between the regulators and the regulated.[4]

There is, then, a tension between deliberation and the push toward quasi-judicial rule making. Is there a similar tension between deliberation and the movement toward synoptic decision making? The answer to this question is long, complicated, and as yet uncertain and will be the central topic of the rest of this discussion. There are so many dimensions to the question that they must be taken up one at a time and then all put back together again at the end.

As a first step, let us recall that in one sense synopticism fits very well with postconsequentialist ethics because it requires that the agencies guide their policies by clearly established public values. Yet synopticism appears to require that these values be created independently and prior to the search for the right rule. For a right rule is defined as the choice of that alternative that will get you to your value at least cost given the existing state of the world. It is incrementalism, the enemy of synopticism, that provides that values are not predetermined but actually emerge from the analysis of facts and alternatives. Incrementalism teaches that it is often more sensible to redefine our goals in the light of what can be done than to struggle on toward preset goals against barriers that upon investigation prove to be insurmountable.

Those interested in deliberation tend to think of it as about goals or values as well as about the means of attaining them. They assume that different interested parties bring to the regulatory process different initial value positions. Deliberators may be synopticists. They may envision a first, distinct, and independent stage of regulation at which the parties discuss their various value positions until they arrive at an agreed value position that is more or less correct rather than a mere lowest common denominator among their individual preferences. A far more plausible account of deliberation, however, would seem to involve a rather continuous discussion of values mixed in with the gathering of facts and the consideration of alternatives. Any agreement on values that does occur would arise out of the problem-solving process. That agreement would be roughly coincident in time with the choice of policy itself rather than preceding it by a considerable time.

Reviewing judges tend to be rather insensitive to this issue of whether values preceded or grew out of policy-making because they review agency policy after it has been made and in terms of whether or not it can be justified rather than in terms of precisely how it was made. So long as the agency can show that its policy is reasonably related to the values or goals that supposedly indwell in the statute under which its rule has been made, it passes the value part of the reviewer's demand for synoptic decision. It is natural for the reviewing court to fall into a certain way of speaking. It talks as if, because the statute was enacted before the rules implementing it, the agency must have worked out the meaning of the statute—that is its values or goals or specification of the good—before it worked out its implementing rules. Thus the court will appear to be making synoptic demands even when it may be perfectly clear to everyone that the agency worked out its version of the good prescribed in the statute in the course of making its implementing rule rather than beforehand.

Those who want the agencies to deliberate can ultimately

make the following argument. Although courts seem to demand synopticism, they do not really demand the synoptic *sequence* of settling values *first* and then looking at policy. They only require that values have been settled during the course of rule making. Therefore deliberators may fit comfortably into one of the most honored traditions of American ethical endeavor, pragmatism, without running counter to the seemingly synoptic demands of the reviewing courts.

This point is important. Those who use the term *deliberation* to mean that agencies should engage in philosopher-like discourse must find some occasion for that discourse. It is hardly realistic to propose that agencies run a kind of continuous philosophy seminar in a back room somewhere. The occasion for discourse about right and wrong would have to be the rule-making process itself. Moreover, if any particular virtue is to be claimed for agency deliberation, it must almost certainly be a pragmatic virtue. Agency values arise not in the abstract but out of the effort to relate the huge body of facts the agency has gathered to the implementation problem it has encountered. Many of these implementation problems arise from the overgeneral or incomplete or ambiguous goals set by many statutes. Otherwise, why should the agency, rather than Congress or a philosophy seminar at Princeton, be doing ethical discourse?

The substance of synopticism may, however, cause the deliberators more trouble than its timing specifications. Both in popular usage and in the court cases, the synoptic agency decision and the scientifically correct agency decision are typically equated. We have seen that the judicial move to synoptic demands first appeared as only a small step beyond hyper-pluralism. The demand that the agency consider all issues raised by all groups turned into the demand that the agencies consider all issues. But the step from total group access to synopticism was also a fundamental shift in the judicial vision of what an administrative agency is and does.

When the courts were fascinated by pluralism, they were saying that public administration was essentially politics and that bureaucracy was basically a representative institution. From that point of view a good administrative decision was one that summated the preferences of the groups that appeared before the agency in the same the way a good election was one that summated voter preferences. Equalizing the access of all groups was the pluralist equivalent of one person, one vote. When courts began to say that agencies must choose the right values and then accurately assess all the facts and canvass all the alternatives in order to choose the best public policy, they were seeing the agencies, not as representative, but as expert. The agency is capable of and required to make technically correct decisions.

The shift to synopticism represented the sixties and seventies reaction against pluralism. It took the form, however, of a return to the initial New Deal rationale for the legitimacy of vesting legislative power in administrative hands—the expertise of the agencies. Except in the sixties and seventies, the expert agencies were no longer trusted to do their expert jobs unsupervised. Courts were to make sure that the expert agencies really acted expertly, that is, synoptically.

Many areas of law are like archeological digs. The law rarely gives up anything. It just lays one layer over the next. A layer of administration as politics had been applied by pluralist judges over a New Deal stratum of administration as expertise. Synoptic judges now applied a new layer of administration as expertise over the political layer. For when courts shifted to synopticism, they did not relieve agencies of the obligation to listen and respond to all groups. But are pluralist incrementalism and synopticism—politics and expertise—compatible? Don't they contradict one another? If courts are going to insure that agencies choose the right values, accurately assess all the facts, canvass all the alternatives, and choose the best policy, why must the agencies listen to groups at all? It is not what the groups want but the right answer that counts. If the answer that would "satisfice" all the group demands is not the synoptically correct answer, the agency should not give the "satisficing" answer.

Rationalist and Prudential Traditions

When courts maintain both pluralist and synoptic demands, basically they are reflecting the American history that we looked at earlier. In that history, the Hamiltonian vision of technocracy, or rule by experts, and the Jacksonian vision of democracy, or rule by the people, may have been contradictory, but they have always coexisted. Pluralism merely substituted group access to bureaucrats for Jacksonian rotation in office. It substituted representative democracy for direct democracy in public administration by saying that bureaucrats ought to reflect what the people wanted instead of literally being the people. Synopticism reiterated the Hamiltonian view that the job of administrators was to arrive at technically correct decisions.

These two contrasting views of public administration are themselves in part reflections of a broader contradiction that has long characterized Western thinking about law and politics. Westerners have long thought about a science of government in which governing could be reduced to a set of rules or laws like scientific laws. Good government would consist of knowing and acting in conformity to these scientific principles of government. It followed that these scientific laws could be incorporated into the actual body of enacted law of particular countries. Good government would then consist of government that obeyed the law. Where government was expected to perform more than police tasks—to do jobs like building dams or cleaning the air—then good government consisted of technical experts governed by the rule of law.

An alternative vision of law and politics stressed the uncertainty and particularity of human events. The conditions that government faced and successful government response to those conditions could not be reduced to a few simple laws like the law of gravity. The human condition was not as regular and predictable as the conditions of the physical world. Good government consisted not of rule-bound behavior but of the exercise of prudence in the face of highly uncertain and rapidly changing reality.

Prudence involves not only uncertainty about facts but a particular approach to values. Those who follow the prudential way recognize that absolutely demonstrable truths about values cannot be achieved. On the other hand, they believe that men and women can achieve some intermediate level of assurance about moral values that lies far short of "scientific certainty," but far beyond mere personal assertion. The belief that moral discourse can lead to sound moral judgment which we have encountered among the postconsequentialists is part of this prudential tradition. People can know enough about facts and values to make sound, prudential judgments about personal matters and also about matters of politics and public policy.[5]

In Renaissance art there is a wonderful representation of prudence as a three-headed man looking to the left, the right, and straight out of the picture at the viewer.[6] Prudence seeks to look at the present in the light of what has gone on in the past and with an eye to the future. Prudence understands that, at any given moment, it must work with the set of limits and opportunities it has inherited from the past to reach future goals that themselves cannot be fully defined now. Our past is not simple enough to be reduced completely to rules or principles. Our present is complex. Our future is uncertain. Mere technical knowledge is not enough. A sense of what is politically feasible and promising is also essential. That sense must be gained by practical experience in politics and in the complexities and uncertainties of the human condition.

Neither the pluralist vision of administration as group political struggle nor the synoptic vision of administration as science leaves much room for the prudential tradition. In one vision administrators are passive reflectors of group preferences rather than persons making their own prudential judgments. In the other, administrators do not need prudence because they can arrive at correct answers. Why be prudent if you can be right?

This avoidance of prudence by both visions is rather peculiar because both the Jacksonian and Hamiltonian traditions of public administration assigned a strong role to prudence. Indeed, one basic conflict of these two traditions was over whose prudence should control administration. The Jacksonians believed that the common people should administer because that was democratic. But they also believed that the common people should administer because administration was a matter of common sense, of the same kind of prudential judgments that common people made constantly in their daily lives.

As for the Hamiltonians, earlier we stressed the technocratic, rule-by-experts element in that tradition. It is certainly there and is the root of the twentieth-century vogue in "administrative science." But there was another element as well. That element stemmed ultimately from Aristotle's views on aristocracy. To the Hamiltonians the most important public administration was bigger and more complex than the everyday affairs of common people. Some of these bigger and more complex affairs would yield to scientific or other expert knowledge. Many of the most important affairs of government, however, would not. Precisely because such matters were big, complex and uncertain, they were best left to persons who had a record of success in dealing with big, complex, uncertain affairs. These were persons of long experience in public life and in the management of large business enterprises such as banks, plantations and shipping companies. In short, "men of affairs" (there were few business women in Hamilton's day) should administer public affairs because business affairs and public affairs required the same sort of prudential judgment in dealing with complex and indeterminate matters.

If prudence as common sense and prudence as worldly experience play so large a role in our traditions of public administration, why does prudence seem to drop out of administrative law? I think there are two reasons, one ideological and the other stemming from autonomous movements in law. The ideological reason derives from the New Deal. The legal reason involves the movement from expertise to pluralism to synopticism.

The New Deal was engaged in a vast and rather sudden expansion of bureaucratic power. It had to fight against strong fears among the citizenry about what this new bureaucracy would be like and whether we ought to let it run so much of our lives. The New Deal's response was to reassure the American people that the new bureaucracy was no threat, that it was just a group of technical experts. It did not make prudential choices for the people. It merely did the technical, scientific, nondiscretionary part of carrying out people's orders. Those orders were, of course, given to the bureaucrats by the president, who had been elected by the people. The New Deal ideal was bureaucratic expertise under presidential control. It left no room for prudence in the administrative process itself. All of prudence was transferred to the president.

Of course, when they faced reviewing judges, New Dealers talked a lot about the need for judicial deference to expert discretion. Expert discretion, however, is not exactly the same as prudence. Rather, it implies that precisely because the expert has a scientific command over the facts, his policy choices should be respected by those who do not have such scientific knowledge.

It is in this realm of expert discretion that we get to the autonomous forces in law. American lawyers appear to be deeply driven by the desire to substitute rule for discretion, to limit or eliminate discretion whenever they can. We have seen that the whole course of American administrative law has been toward reducing administrative discretion. In effect, the judges have said to the bureaucrats: "If you are claiming expert discretion, prove to us that your decision is expert—that it is the correct decision based on scientific knowledge." Of course, if the expert can prove that, he or she is not exercising discretion. Discretion involves choice among two or more permissible alternatives. If experts must prove they have chosen the single correct alternative, they must prove, not that they have exercised discretion, but that they have done what science dictated.

In short, the judges fastened upon the contradiction inherent in the concept of "expert discretion." They said that no matter how convenient an ideological tool the words "agency expertise" might have been in getting Americans to accept big bureaucratic government, when the agencies got to court, they really had to be expert and not discretionary.[7]

At this point we are back to judicial demands for synopticism. For they are the demands that the agencies be expert, that their decisions be the scientifically correct ones. If they must be scientifically correct, there is no room for expert *discretion* as opposed to *expertise*, and no room for prudence either. Pluralist administrators need not be prudent. The groups will bring in all the prudence that is needed. Synoptic administrators need not and cannot be prudent because there is nothing to be prudent about.

All they can or should do is arrive at the correct solution to the public policy problem.

Even if it is true that judges turned to synopticism as a weapon for confining discretion, why is it that this particular weapon seems plausible—that it appears reasonable to command agencies to arrive at correct solutions rather than act with discretion or prudence?

The answer lies in modern movements in policy analysis that began with the rise of "systems analysis," advances by mathematicians and others in probability theory, advances in statistical analysis, and the combination of statistics with economic theory in "econometrics." All of these movements were given great impetus by the need for complex military planning during World War II and then in the age of mutual nuclear deterrence. All of them were made possible by the development of computers.

To oversimplify and vulgarize all this for our purposes, these movements came down to the following teaching. Neither the physical universe nor human life are entirely ruled by simple laws or regularities like Newton's law of gravity. Instead, they appear to be full of random, unpredictable events. The world is uncertain. Observed uncertainties, however, can be reduced to mathematically stated probabilities.

We are uncertain when the double zero will come up on the roulette wheel, but we can say that there is a probability of 1 in 37 that it will come up at the next spin of the wheel. Where exact, objective probabilities cannot be assigned, we can nevertheless often arrive at agreed or averaged subjective probabilities that are good enough. For instance we get a panel of seven horse-racing experts together to decide which horse in a particular race is the fastest and ought to be assigned the heaviest weight. If the weight assignments the experts make keep giving us races in which three or four horses finish close together, they have estimated probabilities closely enough to give us what we want—an exciting horse race. And if one handicapper can do this on her own, then we don't need a panel of seven whose weight assignments we average.

Using probabilities, models can be constructed that take account of the interaction of every probability with every other probability and then generate outcomes to which probabilities can also be assigned. All this will take a form something like the following: if there is a .2 chance that all the attack missiles will launch successfully, a .4 chance that all the defense missiles will launch successfully, a .1 chance that each defense missile will take out one attack missile, then the installation of 65 defense missiles will yield a .7 probability of striking down 10 incoming attack missiles. Each of the probable outcomes can also be assigned cost and benefit figures as can the various inputs that would have to be made to bring about a particular probability of a particular outcome.

In short, uncertainties can be converted to probabilities. Probabilities can be modelled into scenarios of possible outcomes. Probabilities can also be assigned to those outcomes. Costs and benefits can be assigned to all inputs and outcomes. So rational choices can be made as to what policies to pursue. These decisions are rational in the sense that the policy maker can see at what cost he can attain what benefit at what level of probability.

Policy Gambles

If all this were true, and enormous amounts of genius and money have been poured into making it true, then many agency decisions could indeed be synoptic. It would be easy enough to say that synoptic decisions are possible sometimes but not others and that agencies should be synoptic when they can. The truth is that hardly any important policy decision made by government can be synoptic. A large proportion of the uncertainties government faces involve the future actions of large numbers of players in complex situations in which what each player does influences what every other player does. They also usually involve changing economic and technological conditions. So most of these uncertainties cannot be converted to objective, quantified probabilities.

As the recent work of Yehezkel Dror indicates, the conversions to subjective probabilities that are typical of modern policy analysis are largely illusory. Dror argues that even when the policy maker can envision all the future states of the world that might occur and the particular scenarios that might move us from our current state to each of those future states, the probabilities attached to each of the scenarios are almost invariably rather poor guesses even when the most elaborate, computer-aided, modern decision techniques are used.

More importantly, he shows us that there is a second kind of uncertainty qualitatively different from this kind. In many instance we simply cannot imagine in advance all the future states of the world or all the scenarios. All we can know is that we cannot know all the possible things that might happen. And if we cannot even imagine all the future things that *might* happen, we certainly cannot assign probabilities to them all, not even inaccurate, subjective probabilities. Dror argues that we must admit that very, very often what government faces are policy gambles where the probabilities are not knowable. Government faces such policy gambles rather than synoptic situations where all facts, past and future, can be known at least probabilistically, all alternative policies can be envisioned and the probable future outcomes of all alternatives can be accurately estimated.

In other words, most important decisions cannot be synoptic. Dror, however, is not arguing that therefore all government decisions should be incremental. His message is even more depressing. He argues that, in many instances, governments that engage in a long series of small, incremental changes may increment themselves to ultimate disaster. There are instances in which great leaps rather than incremental steps would be best. It is very difficult, however, to assess whether we are in a situation that requires big or small step changes.[8]

The "deliberation" of synopticists might be imagined as a philosophy seminar in ethics and public values followed by a series of laboratory experiments and computer runs. With science serving philosophy, the perfect, or at least the best, decision is bound to emerge by objective, scientific means. The "deliberation" of the policy gambler would be quite different. For what could we ask of the policy gambler but prudence, the grave effort of experienced persons to make their best guess as to what course of future action ought to be pursued given our past experience, our current condition and our sense of what others will do in response to what we do.

Moreover, once we begin to admit that policy must be made in the face of considerable uncertainty, we not only look for prudence but must acknowledge politics. For it is clear that policymakers, faced with leaps in the dark or even with attempting to translate uncertainties into subjective probabilities, will be heavily influenced by their political stances and mandates. Confronting a range of estimates of how many drivers will dismantle automobile shoulder harnesses, a liberal, Democratic Naderite, full of hatred of the American auto industry and passionately dedicated to safety, will choose the low-end estimate that will justify a government requirement that such harnesses be installed. A Reaganite deregulator, passionately concerned about the high marginal costs of getting the last increment in safety, worried about the survival of American industry, and antagonistic to forcing people to do what's good for them, will choose the high-end estimate. He will argue that it is crazy to push up the price of cars (and thus decrease their sales) by requiring that customers pay for an expensive harness that they won't wear.

We must acknowledge that politics does in fact influence the choice of policy under conditions of uncertainty that cannot be reduced to agreed, accurate, mathematically stated probabilities. Indeed, after a little thought, we must conclude that politics *should* influence policy choices. In a democracy, if policy decisions cannot be arrived at "scientifically," how else would we want to arrive at them than by politics. If policy choices must be uncertain and, therefore, should be prudent, it follows that in a democracy they ought to be political.

Here we return again to the notion of agency "expertise" as a rationale for granting the agency broad policy-making discretion. Where uncertainty can be resolved, agency discretion translates into the following proposition: Where a policy problem can be resolved into a set of questions with scientifically correct answers, then a scientifically expert agency ought to be allowed to find those correct answers with a minimum of supervision and interference by reviewing courts. In this situation, "expertise" means scientific knowledge and "discretion" means the power to make *the correct* decision on your own, free of review by others, particularly others who do not have the scientific knowledge.

What does agency expertise as a rationale for agency discretion mean, however, where uncertainties cannot be resolved into questions with scientifically knowable, correct answers. Under such circumstances, discretion would mean allowing experts to make unreviewable decisions on the basis, not of their scientific knowledge, but of their prudence. We have seen that prudence is based on experience. We have also seen that it is precisely the long confinement of experts to a very narrow range of experience that creates professional deformation. The expert suffers from a distortion of perspective that assigns far too much importance to the few special things in which the expert is interested and far too little to those things of interest to everyone else. So the expert is not the best kind of person in whom to vest an unreviewable prudence. Even without this problem of professional deformation, in a democracy, why would we want to be governed by the prudence of bureaucrats serving for life rather than that of politicians whom we elect?

Following Aristotle and Montesquieu, our founding fathers originally established a Senate—which means a place of the elders—to provide our government with the prudence that comes with long experience. The age requirement for the presidency had the same purpose. And the framers took care to provide for a choice of elders through mechanisms of indirect election that were designed to insure that the people indeed chose the most prudent. Ultimately, however, the choice of which prudent persons were to rule was to be made by the people. In the face of great uncertainty, agency expert discretion is another name for rule by a prudent aristocracy. We may not trust the prudence of the bureaucrats. We may not want to be ruled by a bureaucratic aristocracy. If we want to preserve agency discretion, that is, the agency's power to make policy relatively free of judicial supervision, it may be because we want those with a political mandate, rather than the agency bureaucrats themselves, to exercise their essentially political prudence in choosing public policies.

Notions of deliberation or governance that are now emerging in administrative law are recognitions that prudence as well as "rationality" in the sense of synopticism is central to the process of administrative policy making. Often this recognition is put in terms of the claim that Progressives and New Dealers, and synopticism-demanding courts, were making a false disjunction between politics and administration. Contrary to the Progressive slogan that there is no Republican or Democratic way to pave a street, every administrative decision has a political component. The greater the uncertainties involved, the greater that component must be. Most government decisions involve a lot of uncertainty.

This realization leads pluralists to propose that administration simply become politics. The agency should act as an arena for the basic political process of group struggle. Then it should act to implement the preferences of the winning groups.

The Deliberation of Law Makers

The recognition of politics in administration leads the proponents of deliberation to a somewhat different conclusion. They do not want administrators to play the purely passive political role of registering and implementing group preferences. The word *deliberation* itself carries with it an aura of legislatures. It is legislatures that are usually called deliberative bodies. Their deliberation takes the form of floor debate and committee sessions.

Those who stress the deliberative character of some legislatures are usually doing so in contradistinction to legislatures with strict party discipline in which individual members simply vote as their party tells them to without exercising independent judgment. Deliberation is associated with the Burkian model of representation.[9] Legislators are indeed elected and in some sense represent their constituents. They are not elected, however, to mechanically obey the preferences of their own particular constituents. Instead, they are to exercise their own best judgment as to what would be good for the nation as a whole. Representation is not simply a device for preserving democratic decision making when the number of citizens gets too large to allow them to gather together to deliberate and vote. It is also a device for elevating and purifying popular preferences. The common people will elect as their representatives those of experience who have demonstrated their prudence by achieving success at some worthwhile endeavor. These representatives will then deliberate together. Tested and tempered by debate and consultation, their collective prudence shall govern for the common good. Of course, this Burkian model is always qualified and limited by the requirements that legislators periodically stand for reelection. Their exercises of prudence are not entirely freed of the preferences of their constituents.

It follows that administrative deliberators would be Burkian too. They would consult and debate with their fellow administrators to hammer out collective prudential judgments about public affairs, judgments that would best serve the common good. In this context, administrative expertise ceases to be a kind of scientific skill leading to correct answers. It becomes a body of past experience that leads to a better understanding of current problems and a better basis on which to make policy gambles about the future.

Experts bring one of the kinds of experience necessary to prudential judgment,[10] so they are to be active participants in deliberative judgment rather than passive registrants of group preferences. Like Burkian legislators, however, their deliberations are to be framed and influenced to a degree by electoral politics. The elected president will make a certain number of political appointments to the executive levels of the agencies. These politically appointed administrators bring a political prudence to add to the agencies' prudence of expert experience. They add a directly political dimension to agency deliberation. Interest groups are allowed access to these deliberations as well, so that naked preferences[11] are not entirely ignored. Rule-making deliberation is ultimately contained within the statutory and financial powers granted to the agencies by Congress and the partisan political forces that frame its deliberations. In a sense, each agency, too, stands for periodic reelection as it seeks a budget from Congress each year and awaits a new set of political heads each four or eight years.

Prudence and the Fourth Branch

Earlier, we looked at a legal theory of an independent fourth branch spun out of the ideological wars over deregulation. Some of those pressing the deliberative vision of administration are not full participants in the fourth branch movement. They acknowledge as permissible or even highly desirable the participation of the presidents and their political appointees in administrative deliberation.[12] Others use the Burkian administrator, exercising prudence based on experience, as one of the building blocks in creating a bureaucracy independent of presidential control.

In looking at independent fourth branch theory, we noted the key role played by the concept of statutory duty and therefore the centrality of statutory interpretation. Here, too, there are a number of models of deliberative statutory interpretation. In one, a key feature of agency deliberation is a careful, good faith attempt to discuss the intent of the statute. Once discerned, this intent should be followed. The agency would exercise prudence only in choosing the best means to faithfully carry out congressional intent. The agency should carry out the values incorporated in the statute even when it is evident that the statute itself incorporates not the public interest but some special interest that won the legislative struggle. Only when the statute is so ambiguous that it could not honestly be said to clearly incorporate any public value, or even to clearly record the victory of some interest group, is the deliberator completely free to arrive independently at the values the statute should pursue. This model poses grave moral difficulties for deliberators. As honest statutory interpreters, they may discover that a particular statute was indeed a victory for a particular group that was pushing a value which the deliberator's own ethics seminars have discovered to be in conflict with the best public values at which ethical discourse could arrive. Yet, as a subordinate of the legislature, these deliberators should do the best they can to achieve this less-than-best value.

This problem leads to a second model of deliberative statutory interpretation. The proponents of this model usually concede that where a statute gives the agency a clear, precise command, the agency ought to obey, even if the statute's purpose is less than the best. But they tend to emphasize that most statutes are not so simple. Most contain lots and lots of ambiguity. In such instances, deliberators need not go out of their way to cast the statute in its worst light as a mere collage of selfish interests enacted into law in response to group pressures. Most statutes have aspirational elements. Indeed most interest groups engaged in the legislative struggle seek to show that the statutory provisions they seek would serve public values as well as their own. The deliberator ought to interpret the statute into the best one it can be within the limits set by its language.

The first model tells the agency interpreter to be as realistic as possible in examining what went on in the legislative process and to be the faithful servant of the winners there.[13] The second tells the interpreter not to confuse the content of a statute with its origins. A statute may have originated in interest group struggle, but the text of the statute, once it is enacted, is not simply a box score of the group competition. It is a text whose language of values and goals is now set free from, and may be far better than, its origins.[14]

Of course, those proponents of deliberation who are intent on creating an independent fourth branch are inclined toward this second approach. They concede that the agency deliberator must obey the clear command of the statute when there is one, but they tend to think that most statutes do not clearly state their values and priorities. Agency deliberation must necessarily involve value discourse in most instances. A few of the boldest are prepared to go further. They argue that agency deliberators ought to use their interpretive powers to clean up statutes in which some special interest has managed to triumph too much over the public interest or common good that Congress is supposed to serve.

It is difficult to sum up briefly the relationship of the newly fashionable call for administrative deliberation to the dominant judicial demand for administrative synopticism. Both deliberators and synopticists call upon the agency to establish value priorities rather than simply measure the relative intensity of group demands. The synopticist tends to treat the values as preexisting. They are "out there" somewhere for the agency to discover, perhaps in the statute. The deliberator tends to treat the values as themselves emerging from ethical discourse, including discourse about statutory interpretation, within the agency or between the agency, the interested groups, and the agency's political superiors. Values emerge in the course of choosing policies rather than as a preliminary to making such choices.

The synopticist tends toward the view that most decisions facing agencies are technical or scientific ones. The task of judicial review is to insure that the agency has completed the full scientific research agenda: gathering all the facts, generating all the alternatives, and calculating all the probabilities. The deliberator tends to see administrators as faced by many uncertainties that cannot accurately be reduced to probabilities. Agencies are engaged as much in policy judgment as in technical calculation, and so judicial review must be policy review of some kind.

The synopticist tends to exclude politics altogether from the administrative process, which should employ correct procedures to arrive at correct answers. Politics, if they are to be taken into account at all, are placed in the legislative process that precedes administration and in the play of interest groups around the agency. That play keeps the agency honest by constantly pointing out any slippage in its technocratic rationality.

The deliberators leave more room for politics within administration. They are uncertain, however, whether politics means only the "high" politics of administrators employing their prudence in pursuit of the public good or also includes the "low" partisan politics of election-determined Republican and Democrat influences on administrative decision making.

The great disadvantage of the deliberators is that, unlike the synopticists, they cannot specify exactly what decision procedures they want. They must rely on the substantively vague notion of prudence rather than scientific rationality or correctness. The deliberator really begins with the model of the ethical discourse of the philosophy seminar room. That discourse is, in fact, structured by an enormous number of conventions, traditions and usages that professional philosophers have taken a lot of time and much intellectual pain to learn. To the rest of us, however, it seems like a lot of jaw-jaw.

Comparable discourse among a lot of administrators who are not even confined by a shared, rigorous training in a particular style of discourse is going to seem like even more jaw-jaw. To all of this the deliberator can only respond that the picture of right policy decisions being cranked out by a technological decision process is a grand illusion. In the final analysis, wise policy can only be arrived at by experienced, prudent persons sitting down together and exchanging views. In this process, of course, they should have available the best possible empirical information. No matter how carefully sifted and structured, however, that data will not make the decisions for them. Even if we accept this prudential vision as fundamentally correct, it is more difficult than synopticism to turn into law and into supervision by a reviewing court. It says little more than that administrators should think and communicate carefully together.

Chapter Seven

What Next?

Our rather extended bird's eye view of the various movements and tendencies of administrative decision making leads naturally to the question: what happens next? Three basic dynamics established in the past will determine what happens next. The first of these is our shift from demanding that administrative decisions summate group preferences to demanding that these decisions be right. The second is the conflict over what *right* means. Does it mean *right* in the sense of technically or rationally correct or in the sense of an ethically informed prudential best guess? The third is the uncertainty over whether the decision should be arrived at by adjudication or by some far less adversary and formal deliberative process.

We have looked enough at the first, but the second is still very much in controversy and worth further examination. As we noted earlier, the conflict between the rationalist and prudential traditions of administration is as old as the republic. The Jacksonians were pure prudentialists, prudence in the form of the common sense of the ordinary citizen. The Hamiltonians combined the rationalist, technocratic vision of government by experts with elements of prudentialism, in their case, prudence as the wise discretion of experienced men of affairs. The Progressives were rationalists. Government was apolitical, efficient, scientific management. The New Deal claims for discretion vested in agency expertise were essentially rationalistic claims, but because the New Deal reserved a strong position for presidential leadership, the claims of prudence were preserved. President Roosevelt was not technically expert but politically wise.

We now stand at a crisis in the tension between rationality of the synoptic, scientific-management variety and prudence.[1] By increasing their demands for agency synopticism, reviewing courts have made the rationalist vision of administration the absolutely dominant one in American administrative law. No matter what the reality, agencies engaged in rule making must present their decisions to courts as if it were possible to know all the facts, consider all the alternatives and choose the best one in the light of the definite values and value priorities established by the governing statute. The presidency has chosen to try to influence the rule-making process by adopting the rationalist stance of demanding that proposed rules be cost-benefit verified by the OMB's regulatory analysis. So judicial demands are reinforced by presidential demands.

The result is a monstrous catch-22 for the agencies. They could tell the truth. That is, they could openly say in the rule-making record and the concise and general statement of basis and purpose that the uncertainties they faced can at best be reduced to highly subjective probabilities. They could admit that their choices among the range of plausible probabilities has been prudential and has been heavily influenced by the political persuasions of those who won the last election. They could reveal that their statutory interpretations are not correct but a choice among the ambiguities in the statutory language, and that this choice too has been prudential. They could concede that their final rule has been adopted with as much of an eye to ease of implementation as to fulfilling the statutory goals however they are defined. If an agency tells the truth in this way, it subjects itself to almost certain judicial reversal on the grounds that it has acted arbitrarily and capriciously. Courts will say it has not taken a hard enough look, not engaged in reasoned decision making, and/or not met its statutory duties. In short, courts will say it has not acted synoptically.

So instead of telling the truth, agencies can lie; this is mostly what they do these days. They can dress each of their guestimates about the facts, their choices among statutory ambiguities, their compromises to facilitate implementation, and their limitation on alternatives considered in enormous, multilayered costumes of technocratic rationality. They can weave shrouds of data and analysis designed to proclaim the scientific rationality of every choice they have made. If they do so, they also stand some chance of judicial reversal. They are doing so much lying that the judge may see a few of the lies even through the thickest synoptic veils. But it is much easier to eventually win court approval by piling on more and more synopticism than by persisting in telling the truth.

As we have already seen, the first noticeable effect of these inordinate demands for rationality was to slow down the process of making rules. This effect was accentuated when a deregulatory presidency discovered that, even where it could not get rid of a regulatory statute, it could reduce the flow of rules necessary to make the statute work. It could do so by itself making synoptic demands and insisting that the agencies go every last inch in meeting the synoptic demands made by courts. As a result it was actually those who strongly championed environmental, safety, and health goals who first became uneasy about synopticism.[2]

Quite apart from the time delays and money costs of creating appropriate costumes, synoptic demands by the courts create pathologies within administration. They also ultimately short-circuit the very purposes the judges were seeking to achieve. It really cannot be a good idea for administrators to spend a large share of their energies on disguising the necessarily prudential choices they make as synoptically correct ones. Such activity breeds cynicism about obeying the law proclaimed by the courts. It diverts energies from making good decisions to camouflaging them. It tends to shift power within the agencies from those who are really concerned about making policies that work to those concerned with defending them in court. In other words, it shifts decision making from real administrators responsible for the actual operation of programs to lawyers. And it will often lead to a choice of the alternative that can most easily be made to appear synoptic rather than the one that really seems best.[3]

Synopticism and Judicial Review

Synopticism creates an even greater catch-22 for the courts than for the agencies. To understand this point, one must think of synoptic judicial review not in an abstract, timeless, and friction-free world of legal doctrine but in the context of ongoing court–agency relations that occur in real, historical time. In this context, there is a kind of life cycle of synopticism.

As courts begin to make synoptic demands, those demands have two parallel but potentially contradictory consequences. Faced with such demands, the agencies begin employing better decision-making processes and making better decisions. Earlier, we saw that incrementalism can excuse any degree of sloppy decision making. Initially, injections of synopticism improve incremental processes. Such injections put pressure on lazy incrementalists who have been too slow to recognize faults in the status quo, gathered too little new data, considered too few new alternatives and tolerated greater-than-necessary imprecision of goals. They are pushed one attainable degree beyond the most sluggish incrementalism by the demand that they pursue an unattainable synopticism. Most observers believe that the hard look judicial demands of the sixties and seventies did lead to better decision process and product in many agencies.

The second consequence of this early stage of synopticism is a major increase in judicial discretion over administrative policy-making. Confronted by the new demand for synopticism, the agencies are very, very far away from actually being able to do synoptic decision making. They are also very, very far away from being able to camouflage the actual decision making they do to make it look synoptic. Therefore those courts initially demanding synopticism can fault nearly any agency decision as insufficiently synoptic. The courts become very powerful vetoers of agency policy. Indeed, in the course of spelling out what a synoptic decision would look like, reviewing courts may come very close to dictating policy at this early stage.

As synoptic judicial review persists over a number of years, however, aging phenomena begin to occur. The agencies are making better decisions because of synoptic demands. They hire more lawyers and give them more of a role in producing decisions that will withstand court scrutiny. Above all the agencies *learn* how to present their policy gambles as if they were synoptic decisions. They produce the long rule-making records that the courts themselves have demanded. These records are now replete with hundreds of pages of scientific language designed to present the agency's decision as a scientifically correct, technological miracle.

It is this learning process that is the key to understanding the role of judicial review in administration and indeed the role of legal doctrine in social life. It is not true that legal doctrine simply reflects existing conditions or even that it is simply a response to broad intellectual and social movements. Law and lawyers do have a certain degree of autonomy. Administrative law in the sixties and seventies was as much pushed by lawyers and judges from within as it was pulled by outside forces, but those subjected to new legal doctrine do not simply obey it. They learn to live with it, to protect themselves from it, to continue to pursue their own ends by their own means without running afoul of it. In this process they do modify some of their conduct in the new directions demanded by new legal doctrine. They also learn how to persist in the conduct that seems essential to them in new ways that will protect them from legal demands that they find unrealistic and counterproductive.

To a degree, the agencies could move into a more energetic mode of data gathering and analysis, and they did in response to judicial demands for synopticism. Beyond a certain point, however, they saw that synopticism was impossible and that policies would have to be made prudentially. As a result, they concluded that the next increment of resources was better directed at disguising prudential decisions as synoptic rather than at making the decisions more synoptically.

Thus, at the mature stage of synoptic judicial review doctrine, partly through modifying their behavior and partly through investing large resources in disguising it, the agencies have come to satisfying judicial demands for synopticism. At this point, the potential contradiction between the consequence for agencies and the consequence for courts of synoptic legal doctrine becomes real.

At first, when agencies were confronting new synoptic doctrine, court discretion over agency decisions went up, because agencies could never really meet those demands. Courts could intervene whenever they chose on the grounds that the agency had acted with insufficient synopticism. Now courts are confronted with massive agency-prepared rule-making records containing a thousand or more pages of complex data and analysis. In the sixties, judges first made good their claim to increased review because they were lay persons who could act for the citizenry to exert some lay control over technocrats under suspicion. Today, precisely because they are lay persons, judges find it increasingly difficult to exercise review over the highly technical records they have demanded.

For a while some brave judges continued the spirit of the sixties. But how can judges continue to say that agencies are wrong when everyone knows that judges are incapable of understanding the rule-making records that they have insisted be the basis for review? The agencies have learned to produce better discussions and to produce a thick layer of pseudosynopticism that judges are in no position to challenge. Even five years ago, the proposition that judges would actually weaken their power to review by making more and more synoptic demands on the agencies was a highly speculative prediction about the distant future. Today there are very clear signs that we are already in that stage of the life cycle of synoptic review in which the judges must yield to the technocratic defense that they have forced the agencies to create.[4]

Judicial Review and Technocracy Revisited

A second vector of forces leads toward the same result. We have not given up the postpluralist demand that agency decisions be right rather than merely summating group preferences. "Right" in the sixties and seventies meant environmentally sound. Today, without having abandoned that meaning of right, we are also beginning to demand that agency decisions be economically sound. As Americans continue to demand right decisions about questions that used to be scientifically complex and are now economically complex as well, the pendulum in our love-hate relationship with technocracy inevitably begins to swing back. If we want right answers to highly complex questions, who but the technically expert can give them to us? Moreover we have shaped a new technocracy that enlists "eco-scientists" and safety engineers as well as poultry scientists and proinsecticide chemists.

The spurt of judicial activity of the sixties and seventies rode a wave of anti-technocratic sentiment. That wave is receding as Americans are more and more concerned with economic growth, foreign competition, and possible loss of world technological leadership. The notion that America ought to be run by people who know how to do things begins to regain its attractiveness. Judges are among those who don't know how to do things. They cannot now even pretend to understand what the agencies are supposed to have done. Why should they, and how can they, try to tell the agencies they are wrong?

There is, then, a sense in which we now have the worst of all possible worlds. The courts force the agencies to disguise the crucial elements of their decisions, which are really prudential and actually could be understood and reviewed by judges representing the lay public. By requiring the agencies to present these decisions as if they were rationalist, technical, and synoptic, the courts drive the very prudential decisions that ought to be out front and subject to public and judicial scrutiny under a technological smoke screen. So what we get is secret prudence unguarded by anyone.

It is for this very reason that the newest, strongest movement in administrative law thinking focuses on deliberation and governance and, therefore, ultimately on prudence and politics. The strongest suit of some proponents of deliberation is their antisynopticism. They emphasize the factual uncertainties always central to major policy decisions and the evolving, pragmatic nature of the values that should guide, but also must necessarily arise out of, the policy-making process. The deliberators would like to have their cake and eat it too. Those parts of a decision that can be synoptic should be, within acceptable cost and time limits. Those that must be prudential should openly be proclaimed to be so and should be made by prudent deliberators. Their deliberation can and should be reviewed by judges who are certainly not technically expert but can make a claim to being prudent.

Even at their most synoptic, reviewing courts did acknowledge that uncertainty was sometimes inevitable in agency decisions. As we noted earlier, they said that where a decision was at the "frontiers of science" the agency need not be synoptic.[5] Agencies could invoke the "frontiers of science" exception to the synopticism requirement if they could prove to the court that uncertainties could not be overcome and explain why they had made the guesses they did. The frontiers of science exception, however, rested on a rationalist vision. By proclaiming that there were frontiers where uncertainty could not be resolved, it was also proclaiming that in the vast bulk of important agency decisions, there need be no such uncertainty. Prudence was the exception. Synopticism was the rule.

Nevertheless, the frontiers of science exception could now provide the doctrinal route by which courts could move from rationalism to prudence. They have already said that, where uncertainty is unavoidable, agencies may act prudently so long as they explain what they are doing.[6] Future courts need only remove their self-imposed blinders and recognize, case by case, that most of the decisions they review involve major uncertainties that can only be resolved by prudential considerations. In this way the exception could swallow up the rule. Judges could acknowledge that decision makers are usually at the frontier of the unknown when they are asked to make major new policy.

The legal doctrinal basis does exist for the shift from a synopticist to a prudentialist administrative law called for by many of the deliberators. Given that their synoptic demands are actually

beginning to drive the judges out of the judicial review business, there is some likelihood that the courts will take this doctrinal route. To do so, courts would encourage the agencies to
admit that they are doing something that judges can understand
and review rather than pretending that they are doing something that judges cannot understand and therefore should not
review.

Deliberation and Politics

The proponents of deliberation admit not only to the
uncertainty of administration but to its political character.
Administrative deliberation must involve politics at least in the
broad sense that every administrator must be guided by a general concern for the public welfare. The content of such a concern is determined by political values, ideas and assessments.
There is neither a scientifically correct version nor even a con-
sensual version of the good person in the good state. We expect
people of good will to differ about exactly what policies are most
likely to yield even short run, let alone long run, better people in
a better state. We sometimes indicate such disagreements by
talking about liberals and conservatives. Such differences about
the things of the polis—that is about public life—will be
reflected in the choices administrators make. So long as political
views are subjected to the light of open administrative discourse, deliberators are content that it shall be so.

The deliberation enthusiasts are less certain about politics in
the narrower partisan sense of Republicans versus Democrats.
Some are involved in the independent fourth branch movement
and do not wish to grant legitimacy to presidential control over
rule making, for instance. Put another way, they refuse to allow
that an agency's statutory duties might change with a Republican or Democratic victory in a presidential election and a change
of administration. For them the statutory duty is set on the day
the statute was passed and it stays set. Other proponents of
deliberation are willing to take their statutes one at a time. They
see some as fixing very definite duties that were intended by
Congress to survive the changing electoral fortunes of the par-

ties. They see others as granting the agencies so much discretion that Congress must have intended from the first that they would be administered sometimes in Republican and sometimes in Democratic ways.

Once the uncertainty of public policy decisions is recognized, and then the consequent necessity that they be prudential, it is impossible not to see that they must be guided by the political visions of administrators at least in the broad sense of politics. And once that role of politics in the broad sense is acknowledged, it is difficult to see how politics in the narrower, partisan sense could be entirely excluded from the deliberative vision. For being and voting Republican or Democrat is one of our ways of expressing our sense of how we ought to achieve a better polity.

The proponents of deliberation are bent on redefining our urge for "right" or at least "more right" decisions from a technocratic quest to a prudential one. Policy guesses fraught with uncertainty are to be guided by values that are themselves the tentative product of continuing discourse.

Prudential versus Synoptic Judicial Review

Although the prudential view serves as a very healthy corrective to technocratic visions, it suffers from a major problem of its own. It is hard to specify both the procedures and the substance of prudence. How do we know whether a given agency decision-making process was a prudential deliberation packed with moral discourse and a wise choice among uncertainties or just an opinionated mess? At least synopticism proposed a definite, if unattainable, model or checklist of what the agency should have done. If a court told an agency that it had not been synoptic enough, we knew what it meant and what the agency should do next. If a court tells an agency it has not been sufficiently prudent or deliberative, it will be hard to know what it means or precisely what the agency should do that it has not done already. Telling an agency to be wiser is rather like telling a student who got a bad grade to be smarter. It may be true, but it is rarely much help. To the extent that reviewing courts move from synopticism to prudence, they move from a uniform command applicable to all cases—"do everything"—to a standard that must be applied in a particularized way to each case. For the very essence of prudence is particularization. You can't be prudent in general, but only case by case.

Thus court review for prudence would necessarily be highly particularized case-by-case review. And here we finally get to the question, "Who guards the guardians?" with which we began and which we have deferred so long. We have seen that, at least at its mature stage, a technocratic, synopticist, rationalist style of judicial review does not limit agency discretion at the cost of magnifying judicial discretion. Instead it tends to leave discretion in the agencies and leave it there in the worst possible form, that of a disguised discretion pretending to be scientific truth. Prudentialist review rips off that disguise, but it does tend to create vast discretion for judicial guardians.

For how can judges maintain surveillance over agency prudence except by exercising their own? What can they do except demand a more truthful rule-making record, themselves vicariously participate in the deliberations revealed there, come up with their own prudential policy guesses and then see whether the agencies' guesses match their guesses?[7] Where they don't match, it must be that the agency has not acted with sufficient prudence. The judge as senior prudent leads us back to a far more acute form of the "mighty problem"[8] of judicial review, its undemocratic character, than does the judge as senior technocrat.

Of course, one response of the prodeliberation forces is a standard lawyer's ploy. If we vest a prudence review in judges, courts will, case by case, work out a set of rules and doctrines that tell us more precisely what is and is not prudent deliberation. In doing so, they will limit their own discretion. This faith that case-by-case judicial law making will eventually give us a definite set of rules to replace the vague injunction, "be prudent," is not one that is easy to accept. After all, we mean by prudence the particularized wisdom needed to handle particular problems that cannot be successfully handled by the mechanical application of preexisting rules. Even the common-law magic of case-by-case decision making cannot overcome the contradiction in terms that arises if we talk about creating rules of prudence.

If courts are to engage in surveillance of agencies to assure that they have acted prudently, we seem to be right back to the basic problem, and indeed even to the very language, of the arbitrary and capricious standard. For the words *arbitrary and capricious* can be taken as antonyms just as much for prudent as for rational or reasonable. Would a court decide whether the agency has been as prudent as it could be or only strike down agency action when it was clearly imprudent? As in the old days, should arbitrary and capricious be a lunacy test that reverses the agency only when it is crazy, or a test that holds the agency to some positive level of performance? If the latter, how can courts say just how prudent is prudent enough? Ultimately how can courts do anything but match their own prudent guesses against the agencies' prudent guesses, striking down those agency guesses that deviate by some unspecifiable amount from their own?

Here, then, is the purest form of the classic paradox of who guards the guardians. Judicial prudence to make or at least veto policy is enhanced in order to allow courts to watch over agency prudence. Faith in the eventual magic of case-by-case adjudication to bring about court limits on their own discretion is not enough to overcome that paradox for most of us. Faith that case-by-case analysis will finally yield definite meanings to judicial doctrines is particularly difficult in this area given the strange and marvelous turnings that case-by-case analysis has created for the arbitrary and capricious doctrine itself.

Nevertheless, prudentialist review ultimately imposes fewer demands on judges' limited capacities than does synoptic review. For, as we saw earlier, a court that reviews an agency to determine whether it has acted synoptically is ultimately pushed to substantive review. No matter how much it disguises what it is doing in procedural remands, it must finally determine whether the agency rule does in fact embody the correct public policy.[9] Prudentialist review asks a bit less of the judges. To exercise such review, they, too, must do roughly the same deliberative job that the agency did, but they need not determine whether the agency reached *the* correct policy. They need only determine whether it reached *a* correct policy, any one of the dozens that fall within the ballpark of prudential choice.

Prudential Judicial Review versus the Judicial Demand for Agency Adjudication

The struggle between synopticism and prudence leads us back to the classic paradox of enhancing judicial power to curb agency power. It also leads us back to the struggle between those who favor and those who disfavor imposing an adjudicative style of decision making for arriving at major agency policy decisions. Many of those who use words like *deliberation* or *governance* to describe prudential decision making are not just saying that decisions should really be right in the only sense that humans can really be said to make right decisions. Often they are also saying that the best process for making humanly right decisions is not the adversary, adjudicatory one, but the collaborative and mutually respectful discourse that marks the philosophy seminar. In this sense, deliberative is an antonym for adjudicative.

If, however, we tell judges that they must insure that agencies act prudently, how are they likely to do this job? Won't it appear to judges that the best way to insure that agencies meet the very vague criteria of prudence is to require the agencies to adopt the kind of procedures that assure prudent outcomes? What kind of procedures are those? We know how judges and "proceduralists" among the proponents of deliberation are likely to answer that question: adjudicatory procedures, of course.

This tendency will be further aggravated by the anti-deregulation, independent-fourth-branch wing of the deliberators. For if agency prudence is viewed as a legislative-style prudence, then the agency legitimately and without apology may change a rule whenever its empirical guesses and/or political vision change.

Indeed, such an ability to change would seem to be the very essence of a prudence predicated on the constantly changing uncertainties and evolving political values of the real world. In a deregulatory period, however, proregulatory forces are not attracted to such ease of change. The way to block it is to impose adjudicatory procedure on agencies. For with adjudicatory procedures inevitably will come the key adjudicatory pretense and pretension, that a previous decision was the right one unless you can offer very, very good reasons for overruling it. It would be hard enough under any circumstances to persuade judges that deliberation was an antonym for adjudication. It will be even harder if some of the prodeliberation forces are tempted back to the notion of prudence through adjudicatory procedures because of their desire to resist deregulatory pressures.

In the last analysis, the principal problem faced by the prodeliberation, proprudence forces is that they tell a truth that is damnably inconvenient not only for those who espouse an independent fourth branch but even for those who espouse an independent third branch. If agencies must engage in prudential deliberation, then they cannot be rigidly bound by statutory duties. If prudential deliberation necessarily involves political visions and values, then some degree of intervention by an elected president and his appointees and some change of rules as presidential administrations change are not only inevitable but desirable.

Moreover, if judicial review is supposed to insure that the agencies have deliberated prudently rather than adjudicated synoptically, then all that reviewing judges can do is exercise their prudence, too. They must look at the same policy problem, exercise the same kind of prudence and make the same kind of decision. The only way to know whether someone else has exercised prudence is to exercise it yourself and see if you come up with the same answers. If, at some magic point, the agency's prudent answer is different enough from the judge's prudent answer, the judge must conclude that the agency acted imprudently.

How then do we justify judicial review by nonelected life-term judges at all? Why should they ever be allowed to substitute their prudence (which means in part their politics) for anyone else's? Prodeliberation forces have so far not been able to differentiate the kind of prudential deliberation that courts should do from that which agencies should do sufficiently to ease the minds of those who want to cling to conventional three-great-branches, independent-judiciary arguments.[10]

The discussion so far has been almost entirely in terms of the general ideas and theories that are now emerging in administrative law. Readers may feel that they are entitled to see not only what may be emerging at the level of ideas but the hard, concrete "real" law of individual decisions, particularly as announced by that final authority, the Supreme Court.

The Supreme Court's jurisprudence in this area can be briefly stated. Once stated, it will be clear why it is more useful to think about what ideas are emerging than to closely parse the nuances of existing law. We have looked at three major legal phenomena: the transformation of the rule-making process into an adjudicatory process, the judicial demand that agency rule making be synoptic, and the development of a theory of statutory duty resting upon courts actively interpreting statutes and imposing their interpretations on the agencies. Let us look at the Supreme Court's current position on each of these phenomena.

In the famous *Vermont Yankee* case,[11] the Court appeared to call a halt to the further judicialization of the rule making process. It chastised the circuit courts for inventing new procedural rules for informal rule making beyond those required by the Administrative Procedures Act. The *Vermont Yankee* decision did cut off any attempt to proclaim formally the principle of "hybrid rule making," that is, the theory that the courts, through case decisions, had created a whole new procedural law for rule making above and beyond the APA. And the circuits did, to a degree, accept the message that they were not to invent a new procedural quibble to use as a basis for vetoing any rule with whose policy they disagreed. Nevertheless, all of the new procedural requirements that had been invented before *Vermont Yankee* and the theories of "dialogue," "hard look," and reasoned decision making that lay behind them, have been preserved in the subsequent case law of the circuits. Indeed, the Supreme Court has explicitly approved both the theories and the procedures in its own subsequent cases.[12] The *Vermont Yankee* decision provides a potential base for cutting back on judicial demands that rule making be adjudicatory in style, but only a *potential* base.

The Supreme Court has made a major pronouncement on synopticism in the equally famous Seatbelts Case.[13] Earlier we looked at the Benzine and Cotton Dust cases. They certainly can be read as Supreme Court endorsements of the judicial demand that agencies be synoptic although they are not absolutely clear on that point.[14] In a less famous companion case to *Vermont Yankee*, the Court had said that an agency need not even necessarily respond to every issue raised by a group if the group itself has refused genuinely to participate in a dialogue with the agency; neither did the agency have to anticipate all the issues and alternatives that might arise in the future and respond to them. In Seatbelts, the Court repeated that an agency was not obliged to consider *every* alternative[15] and a number of the justices seemed to endorse the "frontiers of science" exception to the demand for synopticism. Yet Seatbelts explicitly endorses hard look jurisprudence, overrules the agency's action on the explicit ground that it was not sufficiently synoptic, demands that the agency do a synoptic analysis as the basis for any future change in the existing rule, and clearly proclaims that the reviewing court will decide just how synoptic an agency must be in each and every rule-making decision.

Above all, the Supreme Court adopted and thus endorsed the technique of the D.C. Circuit of requiring an elaborate rule-making record and demanding that the rule-making record demonstrate that the agency had made the best decision. Like the D.C. Circuit, the Supreme Court was forced to say that it was using the "arbitrary and capricious" standard to test the rule because that, after all, is the judicial review test of informal rule making stated by the APA. Also like the D.C. Circuit, however, the Court used the words "arbitrary" and "capricious" as little as possible and actually demanded that the agency demonstrate that it had come up with the correct rule, not simply a rule that was not crazy.

Particularly in the dissents, but even, to a degree, in the majority opinions, the Court does acknowledge that Republican and Democratic administrations legitimately might make somewhat different rules under the same authorizing statute. But the actual effect of the decision is to use synoptic demands to block a Republican deregulation move against one of the great sixties and seventies regulatory statutes.

So, taken as a whole, Seatbelts reenforces judicial demands for agency synopticism but leaves plenty of langauge that might be used later as a basis for moving judicial review in more prudential directions.

Seatbelts is also relevant to the statutory duty theme because it is one of those rare cases in which a court realistically could order an agency to make a good new rule. The Supreme Court told the Reagan administration that it could not eliminate the existing Democratic rule on auto safety passenger restraints unless it made a new rule synoptically. The Reagan administration disliked the existing air bag rule so much that they had no incentive to deliberately make a new rule badly and thus have it flunk the next round of judicial review. They had to live with a rule they disliked or make a new rule as best they could. They were deprived of the option of having no rule at all and leaving their statutory duty to provide auto safety unfulfilled.

On the key statutory duty question, however, that of whether courts should defer to agency interpretations of statutes or do their own independent interpretation, proregulatory forces suffered a major defeat in the *Chevron* case.[16] The *Chevron* opinion is full of judicial-deference language stressing that "expert" agency interpretations of their own governing statutes should prevail over independent judicial interpretations. And the actual case is one in which, during a Republican administration, an agency is attempting to reinterpret a statute in such a way as to reduce the impact of environmental regulation on economic development.

Nevertheless, *Chevron* also stresses that the statutory language is ambiguous and that Congress had not actually arrived at a statutory policy on the issue in question. *Chevron* does not mark the end of the Supreme Court's maintenance of two lines of precedent, one deferring to agency statutory interpretation and the other saying that the meaning of a statute is a question of law on which courts must retain ultimate authority. *Chevron* is simply another case in the deferrent line. The Court continued to do its own independent interpretation in other cases in the very same term that *Chevron* was decided.[17]

If we put all of these cases and the various interpretations that have been made of them together, what we get is a rather open field. There is plenty of Supreme Court language that can be used as a basis for challenging prevailing theories of adjudicatory synopticism in rule making. That language allows a case to be made for a return to a legislative model of rule making in which the agency is seen as free to choose one or another rule adopting one or another policy on prudential and even partisan political grounds so long as it stays within the outer boundaries set by Congress. There is also plenty of Supreme Court language to support the continued vitality of the adjudicatory and synoptic models of agency rule making and the development of statutory duty approaches. For these reasons, it has appeared to me more sensible to present the current tendencies in judicial review of agency rule making as general ideas than to try to closely parse the opinions of the Supreme Court in order to come up with a definite statement of precisely what the law is at the moment.

Conclusion

We began with the paradox of who guards the guardians. The problem of giving judges discretion so that they could watch over agency discretion had been obscured by a major new jurisprudential movement of the sixties and seventies, the judicial demand that agencies engage in synoptic, adjudicatory processes. That movement denied that the agencies exercised discretion and, therefore, denied that the courts reviewing them did. We may now be partially emerging from that movement. There is a swing of the pendulum from synoptic adjudication to prudential deliberation for the agencies, and the only way courts can check on this kind of agency discretion is by themselves engaging in prudential deliberation, that is, exercising discretion. So we now return to looking judicial discretion straight in the face and asking again, Who guards the guardians? And again we will not answer the question in any direct way, but we can make some guesses as to what our next administrative law is going to look like.

First and foremost, we are going to persist in wanting right answers rather than the sum of plural preferences. The preoccupation of law, political theory and philosophy with values is still increasing. This preoccupation will be modified, however, by our increasing concern for the long delays in making, and particularly in implementing, rules. These delays can only be reduced if we gain more voluntary collaboration and compliance from the affected groups. So, without abandoning our concern with achieving the public interest rather than the mere sum of interest group preferences, administrative law will seek to add more deliberative, less adversary adjudicative mechanisms to the rule-making process. Some of these will be added at the front end, before the formalities of "informal" rule making begin, and some at the back end, as part of the process of implementing rules. In this sense a revived pluralism will flourish, but as a way of smoothing the path for substantively right answers.[18]

Moreover, our beliefs about what answers are right will go from green to yellow. Our concern that we live in a clean, risk-free environment will be more tempered by considerations of costs and benefits at the margin and by a new concern for increased productivity and economic growth.[19] Courts are going to be less inclined to believe that the right answer is the damn-the-economic-torpedoes, full-speed-to-total-purity answer.

A second major development will be the collision of two great movements, a collision whose outcome is very difficult to predict. We are going through a period in which the courts are being blown out of the water by the technocrats, ironically enough, because of the courts' own demands for agency synopticism. Courts are likely to restore their own powers of review by a more honest recognition that agencies do, must, and ought to engage in prudential policy gambles and that, therefore, politics in both the broad and partisan sense have a legitimate role in administration. In this way they will encourage the agencies to give them a prudential record that they are capable of reviewing.

This movement will collide with the long-term autonomous tendency of administrative law to put more and more of what agencies do under rules and to require them to be more and more adjudicatory in process. There has been a long-term march from discretion to rule and from informality to adjudicatory process. That march started by reforming agency adjudication, went on to agency rule making and has shown signs of moving on to the residual category that the APA labels *discretion*. Will this march be interrupted by the tough and persistent reality that agencies must engage in prudence, that most important policy matters cannot be decided by neutral, independent, judge-like adjudication leading to scientifically correct rules? Can administrative law find a place for more reality instead of just for more and more adjudicative processes that pretend what judges pretend—that decisions are synoptic rather than prudential?

I think at least a temporary road block, if not a permanent barrier, in the law's unrelenting pressure toward making everyone engage in the pretenses that judges engage in will occur. I believe this will be so, if only because, without that road block, judges are going to drive themselves entirely out of the agency judicial review business. For unless the agencies are encouraged by courts to honestly acknowledge the huge role prudence plays, they will so perfect their scientistic smoke screens that the judges will not be able to penetrate to what is really going on at all. Review will be reduced to enforcing agency adjudicatory rituals that have little to do with the actual agency decisions.

There may be less judicial insistence on the appearance of synoptic adjudication, less ritualistic invocation of judicial deference to agency expertise, and more frank acknowledgment that agencies must make guesses guided by political considerations. The courts will recognize more openly that rule making is more legislative than adjudicative in substance even if it now labors under court-imposed adjudicatory procedures.

Above all, the opinions may return to the open acknowledgment that rules are, in the terminology used in England, delegated legislation. The very essence of delegated legislation is that the congressional statute which delegates Congress's own legislative power to the agency does not tell the agency exactly what to do. Even if courts choose to do their own independent statutory interpretation, they need not pretend that most statutes issue precise commands or create a single priority list of values with precise trade-offs specified. Instead, courts can admit that the statute really says to the agency, "You may not go beyond certain boundaries, but within those boundaries you are free to do what we the Congress normally do—our prudential best.[20] You may not do X or Y but you are free to choose prudentially among A, B, C and D."

If the courts will again concentrate on this phenomenon, rather than stating it pro forma and then forgetting it as they did in the sixties and seventies, a quite different style of review will result. The agency will be allowed to say, "Our guess is that B is the best solution," rather than "B is synoptically correct."

More important, that same agency in a new presidential administration will be allowed to say something it is not allowed to say now. It will be allowed to say: "Six years ago in a Democratic administration, this agency chose B because B was a good guess in line with Democratic political beliefs. B was a perfectly respectable and legal choice. If Republicans had been in control then, or if the agency's prudential estimates had been a little different then, the agency would have chosen C. C would have been a perfectly respectable and legal choice. And it follows that because, if we had been running things then, we would have chosen C rather than B, we can respectably and legally now replace B with C without having to pretend that B was 'wrong' and C is 'right.'"[21]

In short, courts may come to acknowledge that rules are statutory laws, not judicial precedents. For their own very peculiar reasons, judges may have to pretend that their own previous decisions were "right" and can only be overturned by making a very extraordinary demonstration that they were wrong. But judges need not require agencies to engage in the same pretense. Judges might allow agencies to simply say: "Our prudence led us to B then, so we passed B law then. Our prudence leads us to C now, so we repeal B and pass C law now. We need to show that we have acted prudently now, but we don't need to show that B is really wrong and C is really right."

To put the matter slightly differently, judges have forgotten what rule-making agencies are. They have come to treat them as if they were courts instead of subordinate legislatures. They have also come to treat them as if they were bodies engaged in a true science of synoptic public administration instead of subordinate legislatures. Agencies ought to be allowed to act and to admit that they act as subordinate legislatures making a good deal of law within broad congressional constraints and in the face of considerable uncertainty about facts and diverse and changing political sentiments.[22]

Is it possible for judges who continue to insist that agencies use adjudicatory procedures in "informal" rule making nonetheless to keep this all straight? Can they really consistently see that the rules that emerge from these adjudicatory procedures are not "right" legal conclusions like their own opinions? Can they treat them as prudential choices among an array of equally legitimate policies just as they treat statutes passed by legislatures? I think so. We must keep reminding the judges very often that prudent Democrats and prudent Republicans or, for that matter any two prudent people, are entitled to make different policy choices in a world in which little that matters is certain.

Such a recognition by judges is, of course, not a return to the automatic judicial deference to agency expertise of early New Deal days. Quite the contrary: it is the recognition that expertise does not dictate single absolutely correct solutions to policy problems. Such a recognition will return reviewing courts to the poorly defined question of whether the agencies have acted reasonably. At least *reasonable* will be defined prudentially, not rationalistically. In the end, however, even when agencies are clearly acting within their statutory jurisdictions, courts will be faced with the question of whether the agency's action goes beyond the bounds of prudence, a question whose answer necessarily leaves much to the prudence of judges.

One great danger in this situation lies in the realm of statutory interpretation. It would be very tempting for judges, confronted with openly having to match their prudence against that of the agencies, to camouflage that fact by resorting to pseudo-statutory interpretation. It is easier for a judge to say that the agency has violated the statute than that it has acted imprudently. Statutes are law and judges are supposed to be especially good at law while nobody, I hope, believes that they are especially prudent.

Here again, the stubborn persistence of reality may block the autonomous tendency of law to pretend that statutes have far more fixed meanings than most of them actually do. Some of the prodeliberatory forces seek to persuade judges to find clear statutory policy pronouncements and value choices even when they are not really quite there. Nevertheless, the prevalence of the lottery statute is more and more frequently acknowledged even by lawyers.[23]

A lottery statute is one in which contending forces in the legislature neither reconcile their differences nor fight them out to a clear winner and loser. Instead they adopt statutory language that could mean what any side wanted (sometimes there are many more than two sides). At the time, the sides have no idea what the agencies or the courts will do with this language. They leave the decision about who wins to later agency and court action. Each side has taken a ticket in this agency–court lottery by getting some language in the statute that might be drawn on by the agency–court to favor its position.

Such statutes do not provide a correct answer to the policy

problem against which agency action can be checked. Instead they are themselves the occasion for the exercise of agency prudence. All this is, of course, a matter of degree. Some statutes are far more lottery-like than others. Some agency actions do clearly violate the commands of some statutes. Nonetheless, where a statute which is more or less a lottery delegates rule-making authority to an agency, judicial talk of deferring to the agency's statutory interpretation, or instead meeting the final judicial responsibility to resolve questions of law, is false talk. The real issue is not statutory interpretation, but agency prudence. Courts are probably going to begin to tell the truth about all this more often.

Judicial review in the nineties, then, is probably going to present a more accurate picture of prudent deliberation and law making by agencies reviewed by courts exercising comparable prudence. Courts will more openly acknowledge that what they are doing is using their own prudence to check on that of the agencies. In a sense this is only a way of saying that courts will again more openly acknowledge what has always been the root of American judicial review, that courts are to declare unlawful whatever they find to be *very* unreasonable. When we acknowledge openly that this is what courts do and that reasonableness and unreasonableness are matters of prudence, not technological or synoptic rationality or adjudicative procedures, then we will have done as much as we can do to answer the question, Who guards the guardians? For we know that judges are really no more prudent than the rest of us. So long as we let the judges know that we know that, they are unlikely to get overambitious about substituting their prudence for that of others more directly subject to democratic control.

Notes

Chapter One. Deliberation

1. Two classic works of pluralist political theory are David Truman, *The Governmental Process* (New York: Alfred A. Knopf, 1951), and Earl Latham, *The Group Basis of Politics* (Ithaca: Cornell University Press, 1952).

2. Public choice approaches to pluralism may be found in Frank Easterbrook, "Foreword: The Court and the Economic System," *Harvard Law Review* 98 (1984): 4–60; William Niskanen, *Bureaucracy and Representative Government* (Chicago: University of Chicago Press, 1971); Morris Fiorina, *Congress: Keynote of the Washington Establishment* (New Haven: Yale University Press, 1977); John Ferejohn, *Pork Barrel Politics* (Stanford: Stanford University Press, 1974); Anthony Downes, *An Economic Theory of Democracy* (New York: Harper, 1957).

3. See Carl Tobias, "Of Public Funds and Public Participation: Resolving the Issue of Agency Authority to Reimburse Public Participants in Administrative Proceedings," *Columbia Law Review* 82 (1982): 906–56.

4. Brian Berry, "And Who Is My Neighbor?" *Yale Law Journal* 88 (1979): 629–58; Bernard Williams, *Ethics and the Limits of Philosophy* (Cambridge: Harvard University Press, 1985); H. L. A. Hart, "Between Utility and Rights," *Columbia Law Review* 79 (1979): 828–46; Charles Fried, *Right and Wrong* (Cambridge: Harvard University Press, 1977); John Rawls, *A Theory of Justice* (Cambridge: Harvard University Press, 1971), and "Kantian Constructivism in Moral Theory," *Journal of Philosophy* 77 (1980): 515–76; Ronald Dworkin, *Taking Rights Seriously* (London: Duckworth, 1977); Alan Donagan, *The Theory of Morality* (Chicago: University of Chicago Press, 1977); J. J. C. Smart and Bernard Williams, eds., *Utilitarianism: For and Against* (New York: Oxford, 1973); Amartya Senn and Bernard Williams, eds., *Utilitarianism and Beyond* (Cambridge: Cambridge University Press, 1982).

5. See Paul Rubin, "Why is the Common Law Efficient?" *Journal of Legal Studies* 6 (1977): 51–63; George Priest, "The Common Law Pro-

cess and the Selection of Efficient Rules," *Journal of Legal Studies* 6 (1977): 65–82.

6. James DeLong, "Informal Rulemaking and the Integration of Law and Policy," *Virginia Law Review* 65 (1979): 319–56.

7. Kenneth Arrow, *Social Choice and Individual Values* (New York: Wiley, 1951).

8. The emphasis on discourse is so persuasive that even the casual reader will encounter it in any piece of moral philosophy in *Philosophy and Public Affairs*. See especially Richard Bernstein, *Beyond Objectivism and Relativism* (Philadelphia: University of Pennsylvania Press, 1983), and Richard Rorty, *Philosophy and the Mirror of Nature* (Princeton: Princeton University Press, 1979). For attempts to relate discourse and the concept of intermediate levels of truth to law see John Stick, "Can Nihilism Be Pragmatic?" *Harvard Law Review* 100 (1986): 332–402; Owen Fiss, "Objectivity and Interpretation," *Stanford Law Review* 34 (1982): 739–63; Sanford Levinson, "Law as Literature," *Texas Law Review* 60 (1982): 372–403; Frank Michelman, "Foreword: Traces of Self-Government," *Harvard Law Review* 99 (1986): 4–77; Bruce Ackerman, *Social Justice in the Liberal State* (New Haven: Yale University Press, 1980).

9. See the references in chap. 1, n. 4.

10. I use this term to denote those who believe that legal argument as carried on in litigation is a particularly good mode of arriving at moral truth, public values, and best public policies. See Owen Fiss, "Foreword: The Forms of Justice," *Harvard Law Review* 93 (1979): 1–59.

11. The picture of "deliberation" presented here is built up mostly by extrapolation and extension of the work of the following authors, although none would necessarily agree with it or with one another: Colin Diver, "Policymaking Paradigms In Administrative Law," *Harvard Law Review* 95 (1981): 393–434; Gerald Frug, "The Ideology of Bureaucracy in American Law," *Harvard Law Review* 97 (1984): 1276–1388; Merrick Garland, "Deregulation and Judicial Review," *Harvard Law Review* 98 (1985): 505–91; Robert Reich, "Public Administration and Public Deliberation: An Interpretive Essay," *Yale Law Journal* 94 (1985): 1617–42; Cass Sunstein, "Naked Preferences and the Constitution," *Columbia Law Review* 84 (1984): 1689–1732, and "Factions, Self-Interest and the APA: Four Lessons Since 1946," *Virginia Law Review* 72 (1986): 271–96. Professor Christopher Edley of the Har-

vard Law School is currently engaged in work also highly relevant to the deliberation notion.

12. For descriptions of these two styles and their application to judicial review of administrative action see Martin Shapiro, *The Supreme Court and Administrative Agencies* (New York: Free Press, 1968), 67–91, and Colin Diver, "Policymaking Paradigms in Administrative Law."

13. Herbert Simon, *Models of Man* (New York: Wiley, 1957), 204.

14. Thomas McGarity, "Substantive and Procedural Discretion in Administrative Resolution of Science Policy Questions: Regulating Carcinogens in EPA and OSHA," *Georgetown Law Journal* 67 (1979): 729–810.

15. Theorists particularly concerned with community include Alasdair MacIntyre, *After Virtue*, 2d ed. (Notre Dame: Notre Dame University Press, 1984); Michael Sandel, *Liberalism and the Limits of Justice* (Cambridge: Cambridge University Press, 1982); Roberto Unger, *Passion: An Essay on Personality* (New York: Macmillan, 1984).

Chapter Two. The Growth of Administrative Law

1. The detailed developments can be followed in Richard Stewart, "The Reformation of American Administrative Law," *Harvard Law Review* 88 (1975): 1667–1813; James DeLong, "Informal Rulemaking and the Integration of Law and Policy," 262–356; Antonin Scalia, "Vermont Yankee: The APA, The D.C. Circuit, and the Supreme Court," *Supreme Court Review* (1978): 345–409; Martin Shapiro, "On Predicting The Future of Administrative Law," *Regulation* (May/June 1982): 18–25; Merrick Garland, "Deregulation and Judicial Review"; Robert Rabin, "Federal Regulation in Historical Perspective," *Stanford Law Review* 38 (1986): 1189–1326; Walter Gellhorn, Clark Byse, Peter Strauss, Todd Rakoff, and Roy A. Schotland, *Administrative Law*, 8th ed. (Mineola, N.Y.: Foundation Press, 1987).

2. A. V. Dicey, *Introduction to the Study of the Law of the Constitution* (London: Macmillan, 1885).

3. See Walter Gellhorn, "The Administrative Procedure Act: The Beginnings," *Virginia Law Review* 72 (1986): 219–34.

4. See Martin Shapiro, "Administrative Discretion: The Next Stage," *Yale Law Journal* 92 (1983): 1487–1522.

5. United States v. SCRAP, 412 U.S. 669 (1973).

6. The rule-making or administrative record must also contain all the data and analysis on which the agency based its final action, whether or not it is responsive to particular outside comments. Florida Power and Light Company v. Lorian, 105 S.Ct. 1598, 1607.

7. See Cass Sunstein, "In Defense of the Hard Look: Judicial Activism and Administrative Law," *Harvard Journal of Legislation and Public Policy* 7 (1984): 51–59, and "Deregulation and the Hard Look Doctrine," *Supreme Court Review* (1983): 177–212. Greater Boston Television Corp. v. F.C.C., 444 F2d 841, 851 (D.C. Cir. 1970) is the case in which the doctrine is first announced.

8. See also chap. 5, n. 10.

9. Consumer Power Co. v. Aeschliman, 435 U.S. 519 (1978).

10. Ibid. at 553–54.

11. See National Lime Assn. v. E.P.A., 627 F2d 416 (1980).

12. The Clean Air Amendments of 1970, 42 U.S.C.S. Sec. 1857h–2(a) provides, that "any person may commence a civil action on his own behalf . . . against the administrator."

13. Colin Diver, "Policymaking Paradigms in Administrative Law"; William Rodgers, Jr., "Judicial Review of Risk Assessments: The Role of Decision Theory in Unscrambling the Benzine Decision," *Environmental Law* 11 (1981): 301–46. DeLong, "Informal Rulemaking," notes that the new procedural requirements are motivated not only by pluralist democratic theory but also by the judicial perception of the agencies as technocracies making organizational decisions and by the desire of judges to improve the rationality of those organizational decisions. DeLong's article itself neatly illustrates how pluralist procedural demands blended into postpluralist synoptic demands, for he applauds expansion of procedural requirements from the standpoints of both pluralism and synopticism.

14. The demand is often announced in the form of the "partnership" doctrine, that the agencies and courts are partners in rule making. See Portland Cement Assn. v. Ruckelshaus, 486 F.2d 375, 394 (D.C. Cir. 1973); Henry Friendly, "Some Kind of a Hearing," *University of Pennsylvania Law Review* 123 (1975): 1311 n. 221. It is rare for a court to announce openly that it is invalidating a rule because it disapproves the substance of the rule. Typically, the court will disguise its substantive criticisms in claims that the policies embodied in the

rule it dislikes are inadequately supported by evidence and reasoning in the rule-making record, and it will remand the proceeding to the agency for further supplements to the rule-making record. However, when a court in effect says, "If you are going to try something as idiotic as this, you'll have to make a much better rule-making record," after an agency has already taken several years to build the most complete rule-making record it could, the agency will usually get the message that the court is really striking down the rule on substantive policy grounds. See DeLong, "Informal Rulemaking," 295ff. Courts now look at the "burdens of regulation and the justification for imposing them" (Richard Stewart, "The Discontents of Legalism: Interest Group Relations in Administrative Regulation," *Wisconsin Law Review* [1985]: 668); that is, they do the same substantive policy analysis the agencies do. Garland, "Deregulation and Judicial Review," traces the current judicial proclivities toward substantive review (pp. 530ff.) and notes the judicial tendency to cloak such review in quasiprocedural language and remands for more explanation (p. 571).

Chapter Three. Judicial Power

1. These developments can be traced in detail in the sources indicated in chapter 2, note 1. See also Martin Shapiro, "Judicial Activism," in *The Third Century: America as a Post-Industrial Society*, ed. Seymour Martin Lipset (Stanford: Hoover Institution Press, 1979).
2. See Leonard White, *The Federalists* (New York: Macmillan, 1948).
3. See Leonard White, *The Jacksonians* (New York: Macmillan, 1954).
4. For a description of Progressive theories of public administration see Woodrow Wilson, "The Study of Administration," *Political Science Quarterly* 2 (1887): 197–222.
5. For a recent summary and critique of capture theories see Paul Quirk, *Industrial Influence in Federal Regulatory Agencies* (Princeton: Princeton University Press, 1981).
6. See Michel Crozier, *The Bureaucratic Phenomenon* (Chicago: University of Chicago Press, 1964).
7. See Roberto Unger, *The Critical Legal Studies Movement* (Cambridge: Harvard University Press, 1986).
8. Robert Rabin, "Federal Regulation in Historical Perspective," *Stanford Law Review* 38 (1986): 1278-95.

9. Shep Melnick, *Regulation and the Courts: The Case of the Clean Air Act* (Cambridge: Harvard University Press, 1983).

10. See Loren Smith, "Judicialization: The Twilight of Administrative Law," *Duke Law Journal* 85 (1985): 444; Richard Stewart and Cass Sunstein, "Public Programs and Private Rights," *Harvard Law Review* 95 (1982): 1246–55.

11. See the literature cited in chap. 1, n. 11.

Chapter Four. Regulation and Deregulation

1. On the development of the new regulatory statutes see James Q. Wilson, *The Politics of Regulation* (New York: Basic Books, 1980); Robert Rabin, "Federal Regulation in Historical Perspective," 1272–1315; James De Long, "New Wine for a New Bottle: Judicial Review in the Regulatory State, "*Virginia Law Review* 72 (1986): 399–446; Shep Melnick, "The Politics of Partnership," *Public Administration Review* 45 (1985): 654–55.

2. See David Schoenbrod, "Goal Statutes or Rules Statutes: The Case of the Clean Air Act," *U.C.L.A. Law Review* 30 (1983): 740–828; James Henderson and Richard Pearson, "Implementing Federal Environmental Policies: The Limits of Aspirational Commands," *Columbia Law Review* 78 (1978): 1429–70.

3. Rabin, "Federal Regulation in Historical Perspective," 1285–95.

4. Clean Air Act Amendments, 91 Stat. 685, 748, 736 (1977).

5. James De Long, "Informal Rulemaking and the Integration of Law and Policy," 301.

6. Ibid., 279.

7. Clean Air Act Amendments of 1970, 84 Stat. 1678 (1983) (emphasis added); Clean Air Act Amendments of 1977, 91 Stat. 685, 747 (emphasis added).

8. See Colin Diver, "Statutory Interpretation in the Administrative State," *University of Pennsylvania Law Review* 133 (1985): 549–99; A. A. MacIntyre, "A Court Quietly Rewrote the Federal Pesticide Statute: How Prevalent is Judicial Statutory Revision?" *Law and Policy* 7 (1985): 249–79, and "The Multiple Sources of Statutory Ambiguity" in *Administrative Decision and the Implementation of Public Policy*, ed. H. Kenneth Hibbeln and Douglas Shumavon, (New York: Praeger, 1986).

9. Eli Chernow, "Implementing the Clean Air Act in Los Angeles: The

Duty to Achieve the Impossible," *Ecology Law Quarterly* 4 (1975): 537–81; D. Bruce La Pierre, "Technology Forcing and Federal Environmental Protection Statutes," *Iowa Law Review* 62 (1977): 771–838. More generally, see Bruce Ackerman and William Hassler, *Clean Coal/Dirty Air* (New Haven: Yale University Press, 1985); Richard Stewart, "The Discontents of Legalism: Interest Group Relations in Administrative Regulations," *Wisconsin Law Review* (1985): 679.

10. Probably the most extreme example was the effort of the Federal Trade Commission to set Trade Practice Rules. See William West, "Judicial Rulemaking Procedures in the F.T.C.: A Case Study of Their Causes and Effects," *Public Policy* 24 (1981): 197–218.

11. See Rabin, "Federal Regulation in Historical Perspective," 1297–1314.

12. See A. A. MacIntyre, "Administrative Initiative and Theories of Implementation: Federal Pesticide Policy, 1970–1976" in *Public Policy and the Physical Environment*, ed. Henry Godwin and Helen Ingram, (Greenwich, Conn.: Greenwood Press, 1985).

13. Shep Melnick, *Regulation and the Courts.* See also the materials cited in n. 9 of this chapter.

14. Martha Derthick and Paul Quirk, *The Politics of Deregulation* (Washington, D.C.: Brookings Institution, 1986).

15. Eugene Bardach and Robert Kagan, *Going by the Book: The Problem of Regulatory Unreasonableness* (Philadelphia: Temple University Press, 1982).

16. See, for example, E. Quade, *Analysis for Public Decisions*, 2d ed. (Amsterdam: Von Roister, 1982); Richard Haverman and Julius Margolis, eds., *Public Expenditures and Policy Analysis* (New York: Van Nostrand, 1970).

17. See Richard Stewart, "Regulation, Innovation and Administrative Law: A Conceptual Framework," *California Law Review* 69 (1981): 1256–1377.

18. Concerning the whole regulatory impact and analysis movement see Derthick and Quirk, *Politics of Deregulation.*

19. See Thomas McGarity, "Substantive and Procedural Discretion in Administrative Resolution of Science Policy Questions: Regulating Carcinogens in EPA and OSHA"; Sheila Jasanoff, "Science and the Limits of Administrative Rule-Making: Lessons From the OSHA Cancer Policy," *Osgoode Hall Law Journal* 20 (1982): 537–61.

20. See Richard Markovits, "Duncan's Do Nots: Cost-Benefit Analysis and the Determination of Legal Entitlements," *Stanford Law Review* 36 (1984): 1169–98.
21. Industrial Union v. American Petroleum Institute, 448 U.S. 607 (1980).
22. Manufacturers' Institute v. Donovan, 452 U.S. 490 (1981).
23. Richard Stewart and Cass Sunstein, "Public Programs and Private Rights," 1195–1323.
24. Charles Levine, "The Federal Government in the Year 2000: Administrative Legacies of the Reagan Years," *Public Administration Review* 46 (1986): 195–205.

Chapter Five. An Independent Fourth Branch

1. Loren Smith, "Judicialization: The Twilight of Administrative Law," *Duke Law Journal* 85 (1985): 427–66. The Supreme Court's famous *Vermont Yankee* decision forbidding the courts of appeal to invent more court-like procedural rules has not really cut back on this judicialization. See Cooley Howarth, "Informal Agency Rulemaking and the Courts: A Theory for Procedural Review, *Washington University Law Quarterly* 61 (1984): 891–978; Ronald Levin, "Scope-of-Review Doctrine Restated: An Administrative Law Section Report," *Administrative Law Review* 38 (1986): 283.
2. Martin Shapiro, "Administrative Discretion."
3. Some minor differences do remain between "informal" rule-making procedures, and "formal" administrative adjudicatory procedures, at least in theory. The right to cross examination is more limited in the former than the latter and the right to make oral, as opposed to written, presentations is greater in the latter than the former. The presiding officer at an informal rule making need not be an administrative law judge as required in adjudications. The Supreme Court's *Vermont Yankee* decision, 435 U.S. 519 (1978), did block the attempt by some commentators and judges to proclaim officially that a new "hybrid" rule-making procedure had become a part of administrative law, but most of the procedures advocated by those favoring a "hybrid" procedure are in fact currently in place.
4. Compare Alan Morrison, "OMB Interference With Agency Rulemaking: the Wrong Way to Write a Regulation," *Harvard Law Review* 99 (1986): 1059–74 with Christopher DeMuth and Douglas

Ginsburg, "White House Review of Agency Rulemaking," *Harvard Law Review* 99 (1986): 1075–88. See also Erik Olson, "The Quiet Shift of Power: Office of Management and Budget Supervision of Environmental Protection Agency Rulemaking Under Executive Order 12, 291," *Virginia Journal of Natural Resources Law* 4 (1984): 1–80; Steven T. Kargman, "OMB Intervention in Agency Rulemaking: The Case for Broadened Record Review," *Yale Law Journal* 95 (1986): 1789–1810.

5. Compare Alan Morrison, "The Administrative Procedure Act: A Living and Responsive Law," *Virginia Law Review* 72 (1986): 264–68, with Martin Shapiro, "APA: Past, Present, Future," *Virginia Law Review* 72 (1986): 457–59.

6. Immigration and Naturalization Service v. Chadha, 462 U.S. 919 (1983).

7. E. Donald Elliott, "INS v. Chadha: The Administrative Constitution, the Constitution and the Legislative Veto," *Supreme Court Review* (1983): 125–76; Louis Fisher, "Judicial Misjudgments About the Lawmaking Process: The Legislative Veto Case," *Public Administration Review* 45 (1985): 705–17.

8. The theory of statutory duty is stated most persuasively in Merrick Garland, "Deregulation and Judicial Review," 518–19, 553, 557, 560–73, 586ff; Cass Sunstein, "Reviewing Agency Inaction After *Heckler v. Chaney*," *University of Chicago Law Review* 52 (1985): 678–83, and "Factions, Self-Interest and the APA: Four Lessons Since 1946." See also Chaney v. Heckler, 718 F.2d 1174 (D.C. Cir. 1983) rev'd 105 S. Ct. 1649 (1985).

9. See Morrison, "The Administrative Procedure Act."

10. "Private rights of action" are rights conferred by regulatory statutes to individuals and groups to sue a government agency when it has acted unlawfully. As noted at several points, courts have tended to expand the concept of standing to allow more and more individuals to sue government in order to challenge the lawfulness of rules after they have been made, even before they have been enforced against anyone. In recent years, however, courts have slightly cut back on the expansion. In constructing positive statutory duty concepts (that is, duties imposed on agencies by courts to make rules when they don't choose to make them and to enforce them when they don't want to enforce them), private rights of action are crucial. Most statutes either explicitly or by implication confer standing on those who have been injured by the promulgation or enforcement of a rule. But courts will not normally grant

standing to sue to those who wish to complain of an agency's failure to promulgate or enforce a rule. To do so, courts must find that the statute under which the rule has been made specially provides for such a private right of action. These private rights of action are crucial to those who want to find a way to use courts to order agencies to make or enforce rules. This is one of the reasons that those who emphasize statutory duties often speak the language of rights or "regulatory entitlements." If a statute confers on everyone a "right" to a safe workplace or clean air, it is easier to read the statute as implying a private right of action to compel rule making or rule enforcement. Without such a private opportunity to sue, individuals would have no way of vindicating the individual right to safety or health that the statute grants them. More often than not, however, both Congress and the courts tended to expand private rights of action as means of agency forcing in defense of public values rather than private rights. If an agency were reluctant to regulate vigorously, private individuals could force it into doing so. When courts and Congress were busily expanding standing, private rights of action were congressionally written into or judicially implied into more and more statutes. Today courts have become somewhat more reluctant to read such rights of action into new statutes that don't specifically grant them. Those who complain that the regulatory process has become too adversarial and adjudicalized are leery of private rights of action, because they bring even more regulation by lawsuit and disrupt government enforcement strategies that rest in part on mediation or compromise. Others argue that in reality only a few groups who are continuously interested in a particular agency's rule making actually exercise the private right of action, and they can be drawn into a continuous relationship with the agency that will mitigate the negative aspects of adversariness. See Stewart, "The Discontents of Legalism: Interest Group Relations in Administrative Regulations," 655–74; Barry Boyer and Errol Meidinger, "Privatizing Regulatory Enforcement: A Preliminary Assessment of Citizens Suits Under Federal Environmental Laws," *Buffalo Law Review* 34 (1985): 833–964; Richard Stewart and Cass Sunstein, "Public Programs and Private Rights," 1269–89; Sharon Werner, "The Impact of *Heckler v. Chaney* on Judicial Review of Agency Decisions," *Columbia Law Review* 86 (1986): 1247–66.

11. See Natural Resources Defense Council v. SEC, 606 F.2d 1031 (D.C.

Cir. 1979); Werner, "The Impact of *Heckler v. Chaney*"; Merrick Garland, "Deregulation and Judicial Review," 567, 572–73.
12. See Motor Vehicles Mfrs. Association of United States, Inc. v. State Farm Mutual Auto Insurance Co., 463 U.S. 29 (1983); Garland, "Deregulation and Judicial Review," 573–75.
13. Peter Lehner, "Judicial Review of Administrative Inaction," *Columbia Law Review* 83 (1983): 627–89; Cass Sunstein, "Reviewing Agency Inaction After *Heckler v. Chaney*," *University of Chicago Law Review* 52 (1985): 653–83; Garland, "Deregulation and Judicial Review," 562ff.
14. Kenneth W. Starr, "Judicial Review in the Post-Chevron Era," *Yale Journal on Regulation* 3 (1986): 283–312.
15. Garland, "Deregulation and Judicial Review," 518–19, 553, 557, 560–61, 584ff.
16. Jonathan Macey, "Promoting Public-Regarding Legislation Through Statutory Interpretation: An Interest Group Model," *Columbia Law Review* 86 (1986): 223–69; Cass Sunstein, "Factions, Self-Interest and the APA: Four Lessons Since 1946."
17. Garland, "Deregulation and Judicial Review," 550; Shep Melnick, "The Politics of Partnership," 654–56.
18. Stewart and Sunstein, "Public Programs and Private Rights," 1281–82. Faced with an ambiguous statute that actually expresses a number of values without precisely stating the trade-offs among them, courts are particularly likely to pretend that the statute expresses a single goal or does precisely state the trade-offs. Colin Diver, "Policymaking Paradigms in Administrative Law," 426. Kenneth Starr argues in "Judicial Review in the Post-Chevron Era" that the courts should admit when a statute is truly ambiguous and should defer to agency interpretations, including changing agency interpretations, so long as they are reasonable. Henry Monaghan would turn the statutory interpretation question from a substantive to a jurisdictional one in which courts would ask only whether the agency had acted within the jurisdictional boundaries established by the statute. Functionally this may be equivalent to the Starr approach, because the court would first ask whether the agency interpretation of the statute sought to "bootstrap" the agency into powers that the statute had clearly not intended and then the court would defer to any agency interpretation that did not violate such clear statutory jurisdictional boundaries (Monaghan, "*Marbury* and the Administrative State," *Columbia Law Review* 83 [1983]: 1–34).

19. See Martin Shapiro, "Administrative Discretion: The Next Stage," 1505–7.

20. A major result of this kind of piecemeal, case-by-case and program-by-program statutory duty analysis is that it leads courts to disregard the fundamental nature of the American legislative process in which authorizing statutes for new programs state the absolute or non-prioritized value of the program and then annual appropriations statutes set and reset the priorities among those programs. By focusing exclusively on the authorizing statutes, statutory duty analysis focuses on that fragment of the legislative process that damns the torpedoes and ignores that part of the legislative process that takes cost into account and sets priorities among programs. It is the whole process, authorization and appropriation, that establishes real congressional intent. That is precisely why the fudge language in many regulatory statutes ought to be given more emphasis in many judicial interpretations of congressional intent. That language serves as a substitute for the cost and priority considerations that are added to nonregulatory statutes by the appropriations process. Because most costs of government regulatory programs are shifted to the private sector and therefore are not subject to trimming and prioritizing by the appropriations process, the agencies themselves must do the trimming and prioritizing. Congress inserts the fudge language to allow them to do so. See James DeLong, "New Wine for a New Bottle: Judicial Review in the Regulatory State."

Chapter Six. The Future of Judicial Control

1. See Richard Stewart, "The Discontents of Legalism: Interest Group Relations in Administrative Regulations," 655–74; Bruce Ackerman and Richard Stewart, "Reforming Environmental Law," *Stanford Law Review* 37 (1985): 1333–65; William Drayton, "Getting Smarter About Regulation," *Harvard Business Review* 59 (1981): 38–45.

2. See Stewart, "Discontents of Legalism."

3. See, generally, Philip Harter, "Negotiating Regulations: A Cure for Malaise," *Georgetown Law Journal* 71 (1982): 1–118; Lawrence Susskind and Alan Weinstein, "Towards a Theory of Environmental Dispute Resolution," *Environmental Affairs* 9 (1980): 311–57; Allan R. Talbot, *Settling Things: Six Case Studies in Environmental Mediation* (Washington, D.C.: Conservation Foundation, 1983); Robert B.

Reich, "Regulation by Confirmation of Negotiation?" *Harvard Business Review* (May–June 1981): 82–91; Gail Bingham, *Resolving Environmental Disputes: A Decade of Experience* (Washington, D.C.: Conservation Foundation, 1986).

4. See Barry Boyer and Errol Meidinger, "Privatizing Regulatory Enforcement: A Preliminary Assessment of Citizens Suits Under Federal Environmental Laws," 960; Robert Kagan and William Scholz, "The Criminology of the Corporation and Regulatory Enforcement," in *Enforcing Regulation*, ed. Keith Hawkins and John Thomas, (Boston, 1984); Richard Stewart, "Discontents of Legalism." More generally see Robert Axelrod, *The Evolution of Cooperation* (New York: Basic Books, 1964).

5. See Ronald Beiner, *Political Judgment* (Chicago: University of Chicago Press, 1983); Anthony Kronman, "Alexander Bickel's Philosophy of Prudence," *Yale Law Journal* 94 (1985): 1567–1616; Martin Shapiro, "Prudence and Rationality Under the Constitution," in *The Constitution, Government Regulation and Public Policy*, ed. Gary Bryner, (Logan, Utah: Brigham Young University, in press). The notion of prudence I am setting out here is much less connected to a particular moral philosophy than that which Professor Kronman is currently constructing and is much more concerned with strategies of decision making under conditions of great uncertainty.

6. Titian, *Allegory of Prudence*, London, National Gallery; School of Rossellino, *Prudence*, London, Victoria and Albert Museum. See Erwin Panofsky, *Meaning in the Visual Arts* (Harmondsworth, England: Penguin Books, 1983), 181–206.

7. With my colleagues Robert Post and Ed Rubin, I taught a seminar on discretion in which many of the ideas presented here were jointly developed.

8. See Yehezkel Dror, "Terrorism as a Challenge to the Democratic Capacity to Govern," in *Terrorism, Legitimacy and Power*, ed. Martha Crenshaw (Middletown, Conn.: Wesleyan University Press, 1983), and the various studies in progress cited there; Dror, "Policy-Gambling: A Preliminary Exploration" (unpublished paper). See also Dror, *Policymaking Under Adversity* (New York: Transaction Books, 1986); Hubert and Stewart Dreyfus, *Mind Over Matter: The Power of Human Intuition and Expertise in the Era of the Computer* (New York: Free Press, 1985).

9. On models of representation see Hanna Pitkin, *The Concept of Representation* (Berkeley: University of California Press, 1967); Carl

Friedrich, ed., *Representation* (Nomos X) (New York: New York University Press, 1968).

10. Dreyfus and Dreyfus, *Mind Over Matter*.

11. See Cass Sunstein, "Naked Preferences and the Constitution."

12. See Cass Sunstein, "Factions, Self-Interest and the APA: Four Lessons Since 1946," 293–95.

13. Richard Posner, "Economics, Politics, and the Reading of Statutes and the Constitution," *University of Chicago Law Review* 49 (1982): 265; William Landes and Richard Posner, "The Independent Judiciary in an Interest-Group Perspective," *Journal of Law and Economics* 18 (1975): 875–901.

14. See chap. 5, n. 16.

Chapter Seven. What Next?

1. Careful reading of Vermont Yankee Nuclear Power Corp. v. Natural Resources Defense Council, Inc., 435 U.S. 519 (1978); Motor Vehicles Mfrs. Association v. State Farm Mutual Auto Insurance Co., 463 U.S. 29 (1983), and Chevron U.S.A. v. National Resources Defense Council, 104 S.Ct. 2778 (1984) indicates that the Supreme Court has not conclusively decided between the two. See also chap. 7, nn. 13 and 16.

2. See Richard Stewart, "Regulation, Innovation and Administrative Law: A Conceptual Framework."

3. See Barry Boyer, "Too Many Lawyers, Not Enough Reasonable People," *Law and Policy Quarterly* 5 (1983): 9–35.

4. Gerald Frug, "The Ideology of Bureaucracy in American Law," 1352; E. Donald Elliott, "The Dis-Integration of Administrative Law: A Comment on Shapiro," *Yale Law Journal* 92 (1983): 1523–36.

5. See the text to chap. 1, n. 14.

6. Motor Vehicles Mfrs. Association of United States, Inc. v. State Farm Mutual Auto Insurance Co., 463 U.S. 29, 52–53 (1983).

7. I would argue that those who propose aggressive statutory interpretation by courts are really proposing the same thing when they say that courts must decide whether a particular policy embodied in a rule is "right" or "wrong" in terms of the statute. See Jonathan Macey, "Promoting Public-Regarding Legislation Through Statutory Interpretation: An Interest Group Model."

8. This term is borrowed from Mauro Cappelletti, "The 'Mighty Prob-

lem' of Judicial Review and the Contribution of Comparative Analysis," *Southern California Law Review* 53 (1980): 409–47.

9. See text to chap. 3, n. 14.

10. Perhaps the route to doing so lies in arguing that courts' deliberation through adjudicatory processes can supplement agencies' deliberation through nonadjudicatory processes. Even this argument, however, tends to be frustrated by recent tendencies to describe (and prescribe) judicial proceedings involving large entities and policy matters as regulatory in character rather than adjudicative in the traditional sense. See Meier Dan-Cohen, "Bureaucratic Organizations and the Theory of Adjudication," *Columbia Law Review* 85 (1985): 1–37.

11. Vermont Yankee Nuclear Power Corp. v. Natural Resources Defense Council, Inc., 435 U.S. 519 (1978). Diver persuasively argues that the opinion is antipluralist but not antisynoptic. Colin Diver, "Policymaking Paradigms in Administrative Law."

12. See, for instance, Motor Vehicles Mfrs. Association of United States v. State Farm Mutual Auto Insurance Co., 463 U.S. 29 (1983); Florida Power and Light Co. v. Lorion, 105 S. Ct. 1598 (1985).

13. Motor Vehicles Mfrs. Association, 463 U.S. 29. The Section on Administrative Law of the American Bar Association has clearly adopted synopticism in its "Restatement" ("Scope-Of-Review Doctrine: Restatement and Commentary," *Administrative Law Review* 38 [1986]: 233–90). Merrick Garland argues that this case clearly rejects the quasi-legislative model of rule making and requires that a rule must be right. He himself espouses synopticism ("Deregulation and Judicial Review," 542, 528). After reading a number of recent cases as a retreat from synopticism, Robert Rabin is forced to hedge that conclusion in the light of this case ('Federal Regulation in Historical Perspective," 1322). In a more recent case, Bowen v. American Hospital Association, 106 S. Ct. 2101 (1986), the Court has continued to use synoptic language.

14. See Diver, "Policymaking Paradigms," 426–28.

15. 463 U.S. 49, 51–52 (1983).

16. Chevron U.S.A. v. Natural Resources Defense Council, 104 S. Ct. 2778 (1984). Rabin notes that Seatbelts was 5–4 and concludes that the two cases taken together create a "tension" between tougher and looser review ("Federal Regulation in Historical Perspective," 1322).

17. For example, Bowen v. American Hospital Association, 106 S.Ct.

2101 (1986). Cf. Chemical Mfrs. Ass'n v NRDC, 105 S.Ct. 1102, 1108 (1985). There are various ways of reconciling the Court's two lines of precedent—one holding that the Court should do its own interpretation, the other that it should defer to agency interpretations. See Kenneth W. Starr, "Judicial Review in the Post-Chevron Era." I do not find any of them persuasive. The ABA adopts Henry Monaghan's solution (see "Scope-of-Review Doctrine," 247), but on pages 268–69 of the same restatement obliquely admits that reconciliation is not possible.

18. See Robert Rabin, "Some Thoughts on the Dynamics of Continuing Relations in the Administrative Process," *Wisconsin Law Review* (1985): 741–49.

19. Ackerman and Stewart, "Reforming Environmental Law."

20. Henry Monaghan, "*Marbury* and the Administrative State," 25–30.

21. See E. Donald Elliot, "INS v. Chadha: The Administrative Constitution, The Constitution, and the Legislative Veto"; Marianne Smythe, "Judicial Review of Rule Recissions," *Columbia Law Review* 84 (1984): 1928–68; Garland, "Deregulation and Judicial Review," 521–22, 585. In a major work in progress, Professor Christopher Edley argues that courts ought to recognize openly that agencies legitimately play adjudicatory, expert, and political roles and that some agency decisions are legitimately guided by political considerations. His attempt to reduce the confusion of the administrative law materials by sorting them into paradigms of adjudication, technological expertise, and policy-making is far more systematic than my own efforts here. Moreover, it will, I think, support some of the conclusions presented here. See also Motor Vehicles Mfrs. Association, 463 U. S. 29, 58–60 (concurring and dissenting opinion).

22. Rabin notes that it was the abandonment of the legislative model of rule making in the Kennecott case that started the courts down the road to adjudicative synopticism ("Federal Regulation in Historical Perspective," 1306ff.). James DeLong argues that the old judicial deference rested not on a legislative model of rule making but on a belief in the agencies' neutral expertise ("Informal Rulemaking and the Integration of Law and Policy," 282). As Professor Edley's work, cited in the preceding footnote, shows, courts typically mix together two or more basic paradigms of agency conduct. Although the old deference no doubt rested in part on judicial belief in agency neutrality, it also rested in part on a vision that the agency

acted as a wielder of delegated legislative power and consequently exercised legislative-style discretion within the bounds of the jurisdiction given it by Congress. Judicial review was supposed to insure that the agency stayed within its jurisdictional boundaries, not to second-guess its discretion exercised within them. In this part of his discussion, DeLong himself provides a footnote to the delegation doctrine.

23. Peter Aranson, Ernest Gellhorn, and Glen Robinson, "A Theory of Legislative Delegation," *Cornell Law Review* 68 (1983): 1–72.

Index